WHO GIVES A FOCAL?

Colin Murphy is the author of more than two dozen books, many of which take a humorous look at aspects of Irish culture, such as the Feckin' series, the historical novel *Boycott* (Brandon) and several bestselling non-fiction books on Irish history. Colin has collaborated with Donal for many years, and together they have written and produced several award-winning short movies.

In his spare time he is a dedicated hillwalker and frequently contributes articles to MountainViews.ie. He previously worked as the creative director of one of Ireland's leading advertising agencies. Colin is married to Gráinne and lives in Dublin.

Donal O'Dea is a multi-award-winning art director in the world of advertising, and was the creative director of a leading Dublin agency for many years. He has co-authored and illustrated over twenty books with Colin, and is a keen producer and director of short films and has won multiple international accolades for directing.

Donal's interests also include hillwalking, basketball and cycling, and he frequently participates in long-distance cycling events, including competing in the gruelling L'Étape de Tour route, one of the most challenging stages of the Tour de France. Donal is married to Karen and lives in Dublin.

Colin Murphy & Donal O'Dea

WHO GIVES A FOCAL?

A hundred words and
phrases Ireland gave
the English language

THE O'BRIEN PRESS
DUBLIN

First published 2024 by The O'Brien Press Ltd,
12 Terenure Road East, Rathgar, Dublin 6, D06 HD27, Ireland.
Tel: +353 1 4923333; Fax: +353 1 4922777
E-mail: books@obrien.ie; website: obrien.ie
The O'Brien Press is a member of Publishing Ireland.

ISBN: 978-1-78849-524-0

8 7 6 5 4 3 2 1
28 27 26 25 24

Printed and bound by Opolgraf, Poland.
The paper in this book is produced using pulp from managed forests.

Photograph credits
Wikimedia Commons: pp 7, 8, 12, 17 (Brian Rosner), 21, 23, 25, 29 (Cisko66), 31 Gerard
Lovett, 37, 38, 40 (Maria Delaney), 46,49, 51 (Tony Barnard, *LA Times*), 54, 58, 62 (Geoffrey
Barker), 63 (Rob Hurson), 66, 70, 76, 79, 87, 88, 90, 92 (Robert Ashby), 94 (Shisma), 100,
102, 107 (David Spy), 112 (Michael Wuertenberg), 115, 120, 136, 139, 141 (Tim Dorr),
144 (Andrew Parsons), 146 (Ed Yourdon), 148, 157, 160; istockphoto: pp 56 (agustavop),
84 (Ryan J. Lane), 118 (daizuoxin), 135 (Willrow Hood); Dreamtime: p. 71 (Wivama00) ;
Alamy: p. 132 (Andrii Iemelianenko).

Published in

DUBLIN
UNESCO
City of Literature

Great Irish books
O'BRIEN
obrien.ie

Balbriggan (noun)

Some people may not be aware of the fact but the name of the north County Dublin town was on the lips, or more accurately, on the backsides of countless people all over the world back in the nineteenth century.

Balbriggan, in case you didn't know it, is a fabric, and a famous one at that. It was a finely knitted cotton or wool material that was originally used for men's underwear, which covered almost the entire body from neck to ankles and everything in between. It was napped on the inside so that men's sensitive dangly bits would be nice and cosy. In fact, the boys reported them so cosy that soon the ladies had their knickers in a twist in the rush to get their own balbriggans.

The company behind the balbriggan boom was called Smyth & Co., founded in 1780, which had centralised the local cottage industry of knitting stockings.

Word rapidly spread about the underwear's comfort and warmth levels, and the knitting ladies of the County Dublin town were only bleedin' delighra with all the work that came their way. By the mid-nineteenth century many a royal bod

QUEEN VICTORIA'S SECRET

John Wayne (1907–1979).

was almost entirely enveloped by a balbriggan, including Queen Victoria, Empress Elisabeth of Austria, Tsarina Alexandra of Russia and Princess Alexandra of Denmark. The fact that balbriggans couldn't be removed quickly probably goes some way towards explaining that era's prudish attitude to physical aspects of romance – the balbriggan must have been a total passion-killer, not to mention a serious pain in the arse to anyone with gastric issues.

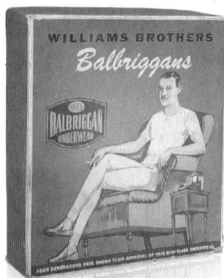

Besides the royal backsides that the garment kept snug, balbriggans were popular with cowboys in the Wild West and John Wayne refers to them in several movies, telling one character to 'put your balbriggans on'.

The Irish polar explorer Ernest Shackleton also liked the underwear, presumably because he didn't want to test the old adage that the Antarctic was 'cold enough to freeze the b**** off a ...'. You get the picture.

Sadly, the original mill closed in 1980, ending a 200-year tradition of neck-to-toe knickers. And so ends this *brief* history.

Banshee (noun)

Phrases such as 'screaming like a banshee' and 'wild as a banshee' are common in America. There are roller-coaster rides called 'The Banshee' (because of the screams the rides elicit) and dressing up as a banshee at Halloween is common, yet most people in the US had little or no idea that the word had Irish origins until the award-winning movie *The Banshees of Inisherin* came out.

Why do they call it the Bansheeeeeeeeeee

The term originates from *bean* (no, not the baked things that come out of a tin in tomato sauce – it's pronounced *ban*) meaning woman, and *sí* (pronounced *she*), which is the singular form of *sidhe*, meaning the fairy folk said to inhabit the earthen mounds that you can see dotted around the Irish countryside. So a banshee is a woman of the fairy mound. The screaming thing associated with banshees comes from the fact that if you hear their keening, which is a loud, piercing and mournful wailing, then tough shit, because a member of your nearest and dearest relations is about to, or already has, kicked the bucket. In some cases, the banshee's wailing is so piercing and horrendous that it is said to shatter windows, in much the same way as a Westlife concert.

Bard (noun)

When most people hear the word bard, their minds immediately conjure up an image of that most English of Englishmen, William Shakespeare. But the original bards were anything but English. They were the prehistoric Celtic poets and storytellers hired by local big shots like kings or chieftains to basically sing their praises and tell them and anyone who would listen just what wonderful, powerful, virile, generous and good-looking guys they were, even if the said king/chieftain was a wojus, ugly, mean-as-shite bowsie.

Bards were also employed to slag the hell out of any rivals. Think of them as ancient spin doctors or PR consultants. The bards have been around for yonks and are even mentioned by the Roman writer Lucan in the first century AD, but their associations with Ireland stretches back into Irish mythology, with the Tuatha Dé Danann numbering many bards among their lot. The original old Irish word is also *bard*.

HOW'S THE CRAIC?

The Welsh and Scots also had their own bardic traditions, but the Welsh

custom faded out in the fourteenth century while in Scotland, bard became a derogatory term for an itinerant musician. The bards were around in Ireland until the mid-seventeenth century, but they faded from existence with the reconquest of Ireland by England, and the decline of the Irish chieftains, so we can blame the Brits for their disappearance. So there's some irony in the fact that one such Brit, Shakespeare, came to be known as 'the Bard', by which time the Irish bards were, to quote the Bard's history play *Henry VI*, 'as dead as a doornail'.

A related term that you'd be forgiven for not having heard is bardolatry, which is more commonly known among theatre luvvies because it refers to an excessive reverence for Shakespeare. While he admired the Bard's works, George Bernard Shaw considered Shakespeare the recipient of too much praise and once described one of his plays as 'stagey trash'. He also remarked that he'd love to disinter the man and throw stones at his corpse, especially as he believed the Bard hadn't engaged with the social problems of his time, as Shaw had in his own work.

But these comments were most likely not because of Shaw's hatred of *Hamlet*, etc., but of the fawning admiration some Shakespearean fans heaped on him. In the bardolater's eyes, the Bard can do no wrong, and no criticism will be brooked, even when it is measured commentary, e.g. the anti-Semitism in the *Merchant of Venice* or Iago's lack of a motive in *Othello*. The bardolater will bend over backwards and do literary somersaults to contrive excuses to explain these inconveniences away.

Shaw coined the term from bard (obviously!) and idolater (a worshipper of idols).

Beaufort Scale (noun)

If you've ever heard the sea area forecast on the radio, you've probably heard this term but never given it a second thought. You might have also encountered it at school when you were supposed to be learning about the trade winds and the polar westerlies, but you were actually dreaming of snogging the girl/guy at the desk in row two.

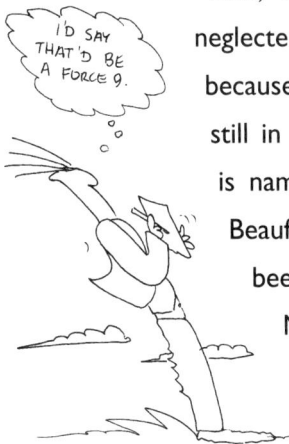

Well, time to catch up on your neglected meteorological studies, because the Beaufort Scale, which is still in use over two centuries later, is named after its inventor, Francis Beaufort. And while he may have been a member of the British Navy and is usually claimed by Britain (what success story isn't, haha?), Francis was

Francis Beaufort (1774–1857).

actually Irish. He was born on 27 May 1774 in Navan, County Meath, where his father was a Protestant minister and a member of the Royal Irish Academy on Dawson Street, Dublin. Francis joined the navy at the age of fifteen and barely before he'd had time to yell 'Ahar, me hearties!' his ship was wrecked, largely due to an inaccurate chart. This experience put wind in the sails of Francis's ambition to improve upon the accuracy of charts and wind/ tidal measurements, and he ultimately became a highly respected hydrographer in the navy.

Up until that point, winds were described only in sub- jective terms, i.e. one first mate's 'it's strong enough to blow grannies off a pier' was another's 'it's strong enough to blow the knickers off a nun'. Francis standardised the whole thing on a scale of 0–12, the higher end describing a hurricane.

An interesting side note: as a respected scientist, Francis was the one who invited Charles Darwin on the second voyage of HMS *Beagle*, a serendipitous choice indeed, and it was on that very voyage that the Beaufort Scale was officially adopted for the first time.

And to finish on a rather scandalous point, when Francis's coded diary was deciphered after his death, it revealed that he was plagued with guilt about an incestuous affair he'd had with his sister, Harriet, between his two marriages. It's an ill wind that blows no good …

Begrudgery (noun)

In Ireland, you can be as successful as you want, just so long as you're not any more successful than the rest of us. But if you do happen to gain financial or artistic or sporting or political or any kind of success that puts you on an even slightly higher plane, you will immediately be the subject of begrudgery.

For some reason, Irish people don't like other

DOESN'T SHE LOOK BEAUTIFUL FOR HER WEDDING DAY!

MUTTON DRESSED AS LAMB.

Irish people getting above their station, as they see it. Why? Well, one possible explanation is that, in other countries, they've been used to hierarchical monarchies for centuries and have accepted on some level that some people will have (merited or otherwise) more success/ wealth than others. Where no monarchies exist, such as America, the drive to succeed is part of their very culture and so is respected. Not so in modern Ireland, where we have a largely classless society, therefore someone elevating her/himself slightly can expect a rapid slap on the back of the head in the form of comments like 'don't you be losin' the run of yourself, ye little shite!' or 'it's a long way from feckin' Chateau Lafite-Rothschild Bordeaux ye were raised, ye manky little bollix!'

But to the word itself. Actually 'begrudge' (v) is a word of English origin, meaning 'to find fault with'. But so ingrained in Irish society is our resentment of others' success, we have added to the store of related words in the international dictionary by appending an 'ry' to it, and thereby inventing a new noun, making begrudgery a word of uniquely Irish origin. Last word to the famed eighteenth-century lexicographer Samuel Johnson, who quite appropriately said of us: 'The Irish are a fair people: They never speak well of one another.'

Beyond the Pale (saying)

In 2010, a US Republican strategist called Karl Rove described certain remarks by President Obama as 'beyond the pale', and in 2008, Barack Obama himself described certain crimes as 'beyond the pale'. What both men probably didn't realise is that unless they were speaking from within an area incorporating Louth, Dublin and parts of Meath and Kildare, they were each beyond the Pale themselves!

A little bit of history. In the decades after the initial Norman invasion of Ireland in 1169, the Normans fell under our bewitching eye, and before you could impale a baby on a pike, they were forming alliances with local chieftains, falling for Irish *cailíní* left, right and centre, churning out snappers by the cartload, learning Irish jigs and getting rat-arsed like any self-respecting Irishman. They had become, according to historians, 'more Irish than the Irish themselves'. This was especially the case in the counties outside the area under direct English influence, i.e. the

aforementioned eastern counties. In fact, relations deteriorated so much between the Normans who had gone native and the English that they constructed a barrier of sorts surrounding this area using 'pales' (from the Latin *palus*, meaning stake) and ditches, parts of which are still visible today. Everyone 'beyond the Pale' was considered a shower of savages by the snooty Sassenachs, thus giving us the widely used term. Those beyond the Pale could also be slagged as 'culchies', meaning rural Irish, but this handy insult didn't make it into standard English.

Nowadays, Beyond the Pale is a three-day music festival in Wicklow, which allows thousands of people (mostly from within the Pale) to listen to music, dance wildly, get gee-eyed drunk and indulge in carnal pleasure with total strangers. Just like their Hiberno-Norman ancestors.

Blarney (noun)

Widely used in the English-speaking world to describe talk that is excessively complimentary and flattering or that stretches the truth somewhat, blarney should never be confused with bullshit, which more describes outright lies. To quote the Irish Fenian politician John O'Connor Power: 'Blarney is something more than mere flattery. It is flattery sweetened by humour and flavoured by wit.'

YOU SURE LOOK LIKE YOU HAVE A BEAUTIFUL... PERSONALITY!

The ability to weave magic words with your lips and tongue is, of course, acquired by kissing the Blarney Stone, which is set into the battlements of Blarney Castle in County Cork. The legend (one of several) goes that the chieftain Cormac Laidir was worried about a forthcoming legal matter so he prayed to the Irish goddess of love, Clíodhna, who appeared to him and told him to kiss the first stone he saw on the way to court, and he duly obeyed,

BLARNEY IN ACTION

particularly as Clíodhna was a total babe. When he got to court, he found he'd acquired the ability to charm the hell out of everyone and duly won the case, and so he had the magical stone set into the battlements.

Kissing it involves bending over backward and slobbering the stone, which has had about fifty million others slobber over it down the centuries. So if you don't acquire the gift of the gab, you're almost certain to pick up something else, like herpes, flu or hepatitis! (Only kidding – the stone is sanitised after every kiss!)

Bloke (noun)

There is good evidence that the term most favoured by our English friends across the water to casually describe a man originated from the Irish Traveller language known as Shelta, which is a secret language based on altered Irish words. There is also a suggestion that it derives from the ancient Celtic word *ploc*, meaning a large, bull-headed man. In Australia the term has even more standing, and 'the Aussie bloke' is a masculine archetype unique to that country, who is at heart good-natured, drinks and swears a lot, works hard, despises formality and is there

to help in a crisis, stubbie in one hand, barbequed shrimp in the other. Bloke is now rarely used in Ireland, and using it in regular conversation is akin to supporting England in an international soccer match – i.e. treacherous. Despite the fact that we gifted it to English, we've abandoned it for our own uniquely Irish version: yer man.

Bog (noun)

Bogs have been in the news a lot in recent years and not just in Ireland, but all over Europe and in the US, thanks to the need to preserve them as a means of fighting global warming. Much of Ireland's share of emissions is caused by our ever-growing population of 7.5 million cows, each farting away to its heart's (and arse's) content. The universally used term bog derives directly from the Irish word *bogach* or *bogaigh* meaning an area of peaty wetland, and Ireland has the highest number of defined bogs in Europe, despite our small size.

The slang term bog, i.e. a toilet, derives from the resemblance of latrines and outhouse cesspools to bog-holes,

THE
BOG STANDARD
SCHOOL FOR
GIFTED CHILDREN

on the bog the morning after six pints, two Jemmies and a curry on the way home.

The prepositional verb 'to bog down' also derives from the noun, and if you don't know what it means, simply take a walk across an Irish bog on a wet day and you'll soon find out.

One other term that may or may not have the same roots is 'bog standard'. One suggestion is that, in the 1930s, most precision instruments were calibrated to British or German (BOG) standard. But the more interesting, though less likely, version is that when toilet bowls were first mass-manufactured, they were all made precisely the same shape – to bog standard!

Bother (noun, verb)

Although it is almost certainly of Irish origin, there is a tiny bit of debate as to whether we can claim it outright. Our only real rival is that it stems from the English word 'pother', which means a choking or smoky atmosphere, or a fuss. Tenuous, if you ask us. But the simple fact is that the word only emerged in the eighteenth century and was first used by Irish writers Jonathan Swift and Richard Brinsley Sheridan, its meaning in their works being 'to give trouble to'. Sounds much more

DRINK... BOTH THE SOURCE AND THE CURE FOR ALL BOTHER.

plausible. Their most likely source is that they borrowed the word *bodhraim* (meaning to annoy or deafen) from their Gaelic compatriots. Another possible source is the Irish word *fuadar*, meaning bustle. A third and more amusing potential source is that it comes from the Irish *póite air*, which means 'hangover on him'. Now, as anyone

Richard Brinsley Sheridan 1751–1816.

who's ever overindulged in Guinness or fine Irish whiskey, that really is a source of bother.

Boycott (noun, verb)

There have been about a gazillion boycotts in the century and a half since we gifted this word to the English language, including famous ones like the Montgomery bus boycott in Alabama in 1955, the Indian boycott of British goods from 1920, the US boycott of the Moscow Summer Olympics in 1980 and so on.

The organisers of those globally famed events likely had no idea that, technically, the very first boycott took place near the tiny village of Neale in County Mayo in 1880, when local tenant farmers ostracised their land agent, Charles Boycott, basically because the tight-arsed bowsie was screwing them out of every penny they had through exorbitant rents, so they duly downed tools and told him to feck off. Pretty soon his crops began to rot, and he had no staff to cook meals, clean his home or do his laundry, so he must have stunk like the bejaysus. He couldn't buy food from local shops, his mail stopped coming and he couldn't even get

a haircut! The tenants' main organiser was one Fr John O'Malley, the local priest, who was keen to promote non-violent resistance, and he was the one who coined the term boycott. The practice took off like a gazelle with its arse on fire, and pretty soon there were boycotts all over the place, striking terror into landlords, and ultimately leading, through the sterling work of Parnell, to the Brits giving us back most of the land they'd nicked in previous centuries.

Charles Boycott (1832–1897).

Nowadays the word is known the world over and is even recognisable in translation: Japanese – *boikotto*, Italian – *boicottare*, Ukranian – бойкот!

(Incidentally, *Boycott* was the title of a brilliantly entertaining novel that got five-star reviews upon its release and should be top of everyone's reading list! Some eejit called Murphy wrote it.)

Brat (noun)

While brat certainly has a distinct Irish origin, how exactly it came to be associated with a misbehaving little gobshite is less clear. Brat comes from the old Celtic word *bratt*, which means a cloak or cloth, usually of coarse material. It was also the name of the cloak worn by beggars and their children. We can only speculate that people seeing these grubby little snappers running about their village automatically assumed they were up to no good, and so the term brat came to be associated with unruly kids, but who knows?

A hardback book was once launched that was aimed specifically at brats. And luckily it hit one of the little feckers.

Bridewell (noun)

Although it has somewhat fallen out of use, until a couple of decades ago a bridewell was a generic term for a prison all over the English-speaking world and the word/name origins stretch back into the distant mists of time, all the way to Kildare in the fifth century. There, in AD 480, St Bridget founded her monastery in Kildare. And you should be grateful, because, thanks to Bridget, we now have an extra bank holiday, meaning you can get legless the Sunday night before and not have to worry about having a hangover in work the next day.

Anyway, devotees of Bridget were soon spreading the word, and Irish monks devoted to her were busy trying to convert the dirty, unholy pagan English to Christianity. In the process, they founded a church smack bang in the centre of what is now modern London, in Fleet Street, in fact, within spittin' distance of the Thames. There is still a church (of England) on the same spot, called St Bride's Church and none other than Christopher Wren designed it.

But back to our London Irish monks, who then

The Richmond Bridewell 1813–1892. Now home to Griffith College Dublin.

discovered a well nearby, which they naturally named in Bridget's honour, St Bridget's Well, or Bride's Well for short. Leap forward about eight centuries to 1515, when Henry VIII decided to build a residence nearby called Bridewell Palace, and about thirty years later the building was converted into a prison. After that, the term bridewell came to be a generic term for a jail, and Nottingham, Leeds, Edinburgh, Dublin, Limerick and Cork all ended up with prisons known as bridewells, along with a great many others in the US and Canada. Incidentally, among the many punishments inflicted on the inmates of all these institutions were flogging, the treadmill and wearing a helmet that could be tightened so it crushed the skull. Ah, God be with the good old days …

Brogue (noun)

Here's a case where you get two for the price of one: we gifted the English language with two terms that are spelled and pronounced the same.

Let's start with the shoe version. This derives from the Irish word *bróg,* originally a rudimentary covering for the feet made of rough, untanned hide. They also had perforations in the upper part, not for laces or ornamentation, but to allow water to drain away more quickly in damp conditions, i.e. anywhere in Ireland, 365

days a year. Originally considered peasant footwear, the brogue (as it became known) slowly became trendy so that, by the twentieth century, brogues were all the rage, complete with perforations that were now purely decorative … a giant step for the brogue from the bogs of Ireland to the boardrooms of Wall Street.

Then there's brogue, meaning accent. Some experts believe that both origins are linked, in that someone speaking with a brogue is using 'the speech of those who call a shoe a brogue'. A more likely origin is from the old Celtic word *barróg*, which meant accent or, in some cases, speech impediment. (Note: the modern Irish word *barróg* means 'hug' and is unrelated.) The word was once used to refer purely to people with an

Irish accent, but now we've got English West Country brogues, American regional brogues, Scottish brogues and Australian brogues.

And as to the Irish brogue spoken by certain movie stars playing Irish characters (we're looking at you, Julia Roberts in *Michael Collins,* and you, Tom Cruise in *Far and Away*), well, they deserve a well-directed, sturdy, size-twelve brogue of the other kind up the arse.

By hook or by crook (saying)

There are multiple claimed sources for this common phrase meaning 'by whatever means necessary', which was first recorded in 1380, but ours has the distinction of having the oldest foundation tale. To be fair, presented here are a couple of the other contenders so you can make your own mind up!

One dates from the nineteenth century and forwards the idea that the phrase indirectly derives from another phrase: 'Foully like a thief or holily like a bishop', the hook being the instrument used by thieving highwaymen, and the crook being the holy bishop's crozier. Sounds a bit crook to us.

Next up is a sixteenth-century petition from the Cornwall village of Bodmin to King

Hook Head Lighthouse, County Wexford.

Henry VIII to be allowed to gather firewood, part of which read: '… where said inhabitants have used to have common pasture, and common fuel … in a wood called Dynmure Wood, that is to say, with hook and crook to lop and crop and to carry away …'. Totally in the wrong neck of the woods, we reckon.

Next up is that in the aftermath of the Great Fire of London in 1666, two surveyors were appointed to determine the rights of different claimants and, you guessed it, they were called Mr Hooke and Mr Crooke. That etymology deserves to go up in smoke itself.

And now, from a totally impartial Irish perspective, we come to the most plausible. In May 1169, the Norman invasion of Ireland began, with ships approaching the south coast towards Waterford and Wexford. They were having difficulty landing due to the conditions, but the captain was determined and reputedly proclaimed that they would land by Hook (Head in Wexford)) or by Crooke (village in Waterford). In the end they landed in

Bannow Bay, about 20km (12 miles) away. Sounds totally believable to us.

Cairn (noun)

When you're dragging your tortured body up an Irish hill or mountain, the slope seemingly never-ending before you, the sight of a cairn peeking over the brow of the hill is truly orgasmic. 'Thanks be to f***!' you mutter as you take those final few steps towards the conical collection of loose stones, ready to collapse in a heap next to it.

If you haven't figured it out, a cairn is a roughly arranged structure of stones, usually in a cone or pyramid-like shape, that often marks the high points of hills all over the world. The word comes from the Irish/Scottish Gaelic *carn*, meaning the same thing. Some cairns are really ancient, others of more recent provenance, and there is general agreement that they are either geographic markers or burial mounds or both. Or, in some case, nipples. More of that anon.

One of the earliest written references is from a 1699 document called *Philosophical Transactions*: '… three great Heaps of Stones in this Lake … we call Cairns in the Irish.'

Ireland's largest one is Maeve's Cairn on Knocknarea in County Sligo, which is over fifty metres wide and ten

The Paps of Anu, Rathmore, County Kerry.

high (over 160ft wide and 30ft high). It is believed to conceal a Neolithic passage tomb from about 3000 BC, which mythology holds to be the tomb of Queen Maeve, who was reputedly buried standing upright facing her Ulster enemies. Clearly, Maeve wasn't one to take death lying down.

Anyone who's driven the N72 towards Killarney or taken the near-parallel train line will probably have noticed two giant breast-like mountains rising from the landscape. These are known as The Paps of Anu (or Danu) and were thought by the ancients to be the breasts of Anu, a mother goddess, so they duly adorned her with two gigantic stone nipples (complete with areolas) in the form of cairns. Anu's eastern breast is

694m (2,277ft) with a nipple four metres (13ft) high, while her western breast is just 690m (2,264ft) with a slightly less prominent nipple, meaning she has lopsided boobs. Still, Anu can probably boast that she has the only pair of nipples in Ireland that, on a clear day, are visible from fifty kilometres (over thirty miles) away.

Cheese and Onion (crisps) (noun)

Yes, the world's favourite flavoured crisps are truly Irish born and bred, and as all Irish people are well aware, when it comes to the crunch, all other cheese and onion crisps are merely a pale imitation of the original (except maybe King …).

When Joe 'Spud' Murphy founded his company on Dublin's O'Rahilly Parade in 1954, he had just one van and eight employees, according to his obituary in the *Daily Telegraph*, in a rare example of the British press giving credit where credit is due. But Joe had plans, big ones. Crisps at the time were either unflavoured or came with a small sachet of salt in the bag, and Joe found these

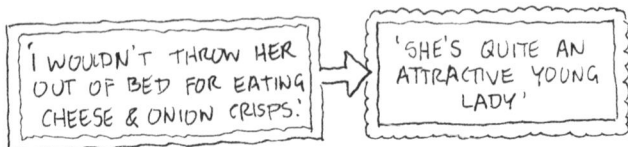

I WOULDN'T THROW HER OUT OF BED FOR EATING CHEESE & ONION CRISPS.' → 'SHE'S QUITE AN ATTRACTIVE YOUNG LADY'

quite insipid, so he dropped them like a hot potato and tasked his employee Seamus Burke to come up with a new flavour. This he did by experimenting at home on his kitchen table. Joe was delighted when he eventually proposed 'cheese and onion' and soon began selling the crisps pre-flavoured. Within a few years, Tayto had burnt the other manufacturers to a crisp and bags of Tayto began to sell by the gazillion.

Of course, soon the cat, or rather the crisp, was out of the bag, and others, especially in the UK, began to try to copy the flavour, and they still haven't got it right seventy years later!

Clan (noun)

Most people would probably imagine this is a word of Scottish origin, given the importance of clans and clan politics in Scottish history, but no, there's about as much truth to that as there is to Nessie.

The word clan derives from the old Irish word *cland*, which evolved to become the Gaelic word *clann* by the sixteenth century, meaning children or offspring. The Scots then borrowed the word and never gave it back. Feckin' typical.

To be a true member of a clan, by the way, besides having the same surname, you had to be directly linked by a bloodline all the way back into the mists of time to the original clan chieftain. Otherwise, you were just a hanger-on. While the Scottish clan system still exists (minus the political angle), the Irish clans all but disappeared with the Tudor conquest.

Clock (noun)

We're going to set the record straight on the origin of clock, and it's about time. If you consult various sources, they'll probably tell you that the word originates from the medieval Latin word *clocca,* meaning bell, or from the Dutch *klok* or the French *cloche.* But all those theories are cuckoo, because the medieval Latin word itself originated from the old Irish *clocc.* We're not winding you up here.

Not only that, but the word was then spread around Europe by Irish monks who were renowned in their day for enlightening the poor continental eejits who were living through the Dark Ages. In fact, our holy Joe monks were regarded as the leading experts in the field of chronology, and used their skills to accurately predict the date for Easter in any given year.

Ahead of our feckin' time, we were.

HAVE YOU GOT THE TIME, FATHER?

I COULD MAKE SOME FOR YOU!!!

Colleen (noun)

It's pretty obvious where the word colleen originated – it's a direct anglicisation of the Irish word *cailín*, meaning girl. It's also easy to see how the term entered the English language, which came about through Irish emigrants, particularly to the US, using the term casually among their new American friends who then spelled it as they heard it.

But its generic use as a term for a young woman really only became widespread in the 1920s, thanks to Hollywood's promotion of a new starlet, one Colleen Moore, a beautiful young Irish American actress who was a massive star in her day, and although largely forgotten now, enjoyed success on the level of, say, Scarlett Johansson or Reese Witherspoon.

Colleen was what was known as a flapper, which sounds suspiciously like something you'd use to spice up your sex life, but in fact was a term for young women in the era who were famous – or infamous – for their risqué lifestyles and open flaunting of what was considered respectable. They

did things like wear short skirts, they openly smoked and drank alcohol, wore excessive make-up, drove cars and had a relaxed attitude to sex – shocking! So basically, they were trailblazers for the millions of women who enjoy all such indulgences nowadays.

Anyway, Colleen was regarded as so beautiful and was so admired, Hollywood continued to use the terms colleen and coleen when referencing other upcoming starlets and slowly the use of the word became widespread.

Incidentally, when Colleen Moore left the movie business, she then morphed into a successful businesswoman, became a partner in the investment company Merrill-Lynch, released several bestselling books, and ended her days as a very wealthy and successful woman. She was one colleen ahead of her time.

Corrie (noun)

Ask most people what a corrie is and they'll probably tell you that it's a soap opera on ITV, but no, this has nothing to do with Ken Barlow or The Rover's Return pub. A corrie, as any hillwalker or geography teacher will tell you, is a giant hollow in the side of a mountain that has formed as a result of glacial erosion, often containing a lake – basically they look like gigantic three-sided natural arenas. Examples of corries are Upper and Lower Lough Bray in Wicklow, Coomshingaun Lough, County Waterford or Gougane Barra in County Cork. There are gazillions of corries around Ireland and they're usually quite beautiful places.

The word is used around the world to describe this type of feature, and it derives from the Irish/Scots Gaelic term *coire,* meaning cauldron or hollow.

I KNOW THESE MOUNTAINS LIKE THE BACK OF MY HAND.

Crag, Craggy (noun, adj.)

More geographical/geological stuff, a crag is a steep or rugged rock face, often on the coastline. But there are literally thousands of crags around the island, from Glendalough in Wicklow to the Burren in Clare to Donegal's spectacular Slieve League. Beloved of rock climbers, who relish the challenge of defying the possibility of plummeting to earth and exploding like a tomato, crags were formed tens of millions of years ago, or in some cases hundreds of millions of years ago. Crag Cave in Kerry takes its name from the term.

HANG ON. I LEFT MY PHONE BACK AT THE CAR

Crag has become a universal term, used to describe these geological features all over the planet, and the word comes from the Old Irish word *crec* meaning rock, or *carrac* meaning cliff. The modern Irish word for rock, *carraig,* is not too dissimilar.

Incidentally the name Craig derives directly from the term and means 'dweller by the steep rocks'.

Stalagmites, Crag Cave, County Kerry.

Crag has also given us the adjective craggy to describe something rugged and full of crags, like some ageing movie and rock stars' faces before the plastic surgery.

Cream cracker (noun)

They may be crackly yet they're anything but creamy, and they are known the world over as one of most versatile snack foods – and their global fame began in the kitchen of a man called Joseph Haughton in Dublin around 1885. Nothing much is known about Joseph, except that he may have hailed from Rathmines. He then approached the Jacob brothers, originally from Waterford but by then operating in the capital city, pitched them his invention and, before you know it, sales had gone, well, crackers.

The Jacob's cream crackers' fame spread faster than cream cheese and nowadays their fan base extends through Europe, Asia, North and South America, South Africa and India. You've probably never wondered why they're called *cream* crackers, and who would blame you, but anyway it's from the way the dough mixture is creamed during manufacture, and the reason for the matrix of tiny holes is to prevent the cracker from puffing up too much during baking.

Depending on where you are in the world, your cream cracker topping can range from raw octopus to strawberries and ricotta, from guacamole to banana and chocolate, or to butter and jam (or a combination of all of the above).

They can also be used in a challenging party game – how many cream crackers can you swallow in one minute without any water or other libation? You'll be lucky if you get past one!

THESE CREAM
CRACKERS TAKE
← THE BISCUIT.

Croquet (noun)

Say the word croquet and it conjures up images of gentlemen with handlebar moustaches and ladies in long dresses clutching wooden mallets trying to hit a ball through a tiny wooden hoop, all looking very, very British and like a bunch of ridiculous gobshites. Yet the word sounds distinctly French, and indeed there is one theory that it evolved in the seventeenth century from the French game of *paille-maille* (ball-mallet). In fact, the London street known as Pall Mall took its name from this game having been played there.

While those games bore a resemblance to croquet, they lacked definitive rules and the distinctive croquet stroke – the mallet held in front of the body and in line with the ball and hoop. But there is general agreement that the modern rules of the game originated in Ireland

BACK IN 1834 CROQUET WAS TAKEN MORE SERIOUSLY.

in the early eighteenth century, or at least so say Croquet England, and who are we to argue with them? There is a record of a similar game called *crookey* (now we're starting to sound Irish!) being played in County Louth in 1834. By the following year, this game had reached Kingstown (now Dún Laoghaire) where the well-heeled residents changed the name to croquet, probably because the French-sounding word made it appear posher. An early croquet historian (yes, there is such a thing), one Dr Richard Prior, stated in his history that: '... one thing only is certain: it is from Ireland that croquet came to England and it was on the lawn of Lord Lonsdale that it was first played in this country in 1851.'

Cry over spilt milk (saying)

IT'S NOT SPILT MILK,
IT'S ME FECKIN' PINT.

This common phrase, meaning 'to whinge about events that can't be undone', and which is still widely used to this day, was coined in 1738 by none other than Jonathan Swift, who used the phrase in his work *Polite Conversation*, which basically slagged the hell out of the banality of conversation of the upper classes in the eighteenth century. The conversation in question goes like this:

Lady Answerall: Lord, Madam, How
   came you to break your Cup?
Lady Smart: I can't help it, if I would cry my Eyes out.
Miss: Why, sell it, Madam, and buy a new
   one with some of the Money.
Colonel: 'Tis a Folly to cry for spilt Milk.

Dig/Twig (verb)

Not what you do with a shovel, but here in the slang sense of 'I dig' i.e. 'I understand'. Okay, we admit the jury is still out on this one, and probably will be out forever. If you read some etymologists, they'll tell you

GROOVY. I DIG IT, MAN.

that the source is unknown, others will tell you that it has its roots in African American vernacular, and in the case of 'twig', some even claim that it arose from the action of a hunter stepping on a twig and thereby alerting the prey. But there is also a case to be made that dig and twig (i.e. to catch on) came from the Irish word *tuig*, meaning 'understand'. *An dtuigeann tú?*

Donnybrook (noun)

Although not widely used in Ireland, a donnybrook is a well-known term in the US and Australia for a bunch of eejits battering the livin' bejaysus out of each other.

The term arose as a result of the annual two-week Donnybrook Fair, which, believe it or not, had a history stretching all the way back to 1204, when the English King John granted it a charter. The first six centuries of fairs were mostly peaceful affairs, with people trading livestock and agricultural produce with a bit of hooleying and drinking thrown in – sort of like a medieval National Ploughing Championships – until the beginning of the nineteenth century, when things started to go to the dogs. The trading in bullocks and spuds became less important than the trading in blows of shillelaghs and bottles, usually as a result of excessive drink taken. There are also suggestions in contemporary reports of other vices being

DID YOU HAVE A NICE TIME AT THE FAIR, DEAR?

indulged. Here's a report from the *Parliamentary Gazetteer* from August 1845:

> It was for generations a perfect prodigy of moral horrors – a concentration of disgrace upon, not Ireland alone, but civilized Europe. It far surpassed all other fairs in the multitude and grossness of its disgusting incidents of vice; and, in general, it exhibited such continuous scenes of riot, bloodshed, debauchery, and brutality … This was by day; the orgies of the night may better be imagined than described.

Things usually started off with a couple of men getting into a fight, either through some argument or sometimes as a 'sporting' bout of fisticuffs. Drunken onlookers would then become involved, and more drunken onlookers would then start boxing the head off the other drunken

Donnybrook Fair by Erskine Nicol (1859).

onlookers until the whole thing spiralled into a gigantic melee involving hundreds of fellas battering the shite out of each other. It must have been a sight to see!

Eventually outraged locals and the Catholic Church got together and brought the whole thing to an end in 1855. Spoilsports.

Incidentally, the fair took place on the site of what is now Donnybrook Rugby Stadium, where drunken crowds nowadays gather to watch fellas batter the shite out of each other on the rugby field.

Dornick (noun)

The famed author of hard-boiled 1930s detective fiction, Dashiell Hammett, has a character in his novel *After the Thin Man* relate how he received a message: 'Somebody wrapped it around a dornick and heaved it through my window.' Which tells us that people in San Francisco,

WHAT EXACTLY
IS A DORNICK
SUPPOSED TO
LOOK LIKE, HUH?

the novel's setting, were clearly familiar with this word that means a stone, usually small enough to throw. Most Irish people probably wouldn't have a clue what it meant, despite the fact that it almost certainly derives from the Irish word *dornóg*, also meaning a small, round stone.

The term is common in the US and actually several places in the states of Arkansas, Oklahoma and Pennsylvania take their name from it.

Mind you, the Rolling Dornicks doesn't have quite the same ring to it.

Dracula (noun)

Here's one you can sink your teeth into, because Bram Stoker's 1897 creation, like the fictional character, seems to have an eternal life, judging by how often a new book, play, movie or TV series is produced concerning him. The word 'vampire' immediately prompts the name 'Dracula', no matter which part of the world is your haunt. And every Halloween there is a renewed surge in interest, as though the world was trying to bleed the character dry.

FANCY A PINT?
BLOOD BANK

And here's some stuff you probably didn't know about our neck-chomping villain and his creator. Although bats had some association with vampires thanks to the existence of the vampire bat, Bram Stoker giving Dracula the ability to morph into a bat made the connection indelible. The other vampire stuff – his fear of garlic, crucifixes and sunshine – were all either popularised or created by Bram.

People who study the work often identify strong homo-sexual themes – Dracula biting a man's neck for example, and when three beautiful female vampires descend on the character of Jonathan Harker, proclaiming 'there are kisses for us all', Dracula bursts in and shouts 'the man belongs to me!' Despite him being married, academics suspect

Bram Stoker (1847–1912).

Bram was as gay as Christmas and possibly had flings with both Oscar Wilde and Walt Whitman.

As to the inspiration, there are several theories. One is that Dracula is based on the fifteenth-century Vlad the Impaler of Transylvania, who reputedly impaled thousands of men, women and children on stakes during his reign. Lovely guy. He was also known as Vlad Dracula (meaning 'son of the devil', and this is where Bram found the name and introduced it to the wider world). Another source was possibly the seventeenth-century Hungarian noblewoman Countess Elizabeth Báthory, who allegedly murdered hundreds of young women and is said to have bathed in the blood of virgins. Talk about a bloodbath! And lastly there's the Irish legend of Abhartach, an evil vampire-like dwarf who rises from the grave to drink the blood of the living. Take your pick.

Incidentally, there have been about a hundred and twenty movies or TV series about Dracula, not including movies of the blue variety, which include such timeless classics as *Lust at First Bite*, *Dracula's Love Bites*, *Lust for Dracula* and *Dracula Sucks*!

Drumlin (noun)

Just in case your geological terminology isn't up to scratch, a drumlin is the word used worldwide to describe a low, oval hill that was formed by the movement of glacial ice sheets, the resultant hill being aligned with the direction of the glacier's movement. Think of them like a giant hard-boiled egg half buried in the ground. A good example is the islands of Clew Bay, one of which, Dorinish, was once owned by John Lennon, and where he planned to retire. Sadly, John ended his days on Manhattan Island, which coincidentally also has numerous drumlins. In folklore, drumlin mounds were believed to be the homes of the fairy folk.

The word derives from the Irish word *druim,* meaning rounded hill, or *droimnín,* meaning little ridge.

John Lennon (1940–1980).

Duty Free (noun)

There have been countless billions of litres of cheap vodka and whiskey drunk, even more billions of cheap smokes smoked, and a veritable ocean of cheap perfume sniffed since the world's first duty-free shop opened its doors. And who do all those happy drinkers, smokers and nice-smelling ladies and gents have to thank?

Yes, Ireland gave all those cheaply acquired hangovers, smokers' coughs and overpowering aromas to the world back in 1947 when Shannon Airport opened the very first duty-free shop on the planet. Or to be more accurate, a man called Brendan O'Regan did when he invented the concept. Within two decades of Shannon's duty-free shop opening its doors, the term had appeared in virtually every port and airport on the planet, to the joy of ganseyloads of grateful tax-dodging customers.

FAIR PLAY TO YE, BRENDAN.

Brendan was a brilliant businessman who was also the driving force behind the Shannon Industrial Zone and the initiative to turn Bunratty Castle into a major

I'M NOT AS THINK AS YOU DRUNK I AM!

tourist attraction. If that wasn't enough, he also created Co-operation Ireland to foster peace and reconciliation on the island. He truly went above and beyond the call of duty-free.

Electron (noun)

Offaly man George J. Stoney (1826–1911) gave the world of physics the term electron in 1891. An electron is not an election poster for a candidate called Ronald (groan!), but the smallest stable sub-atomic particle known. It's small. In fact, it's really, really, go-way-outta-dat small. A single kilogram (2.2lb) of just electrons (a scientific impossibility, by the way) would contain roughly 90,000,000,000 000,000,000,000,000,000, give or take a gazillion. An electron has a negative charge and a proton has a positive charge and, if you wanted to make personal contact with some electrons, you could grab a live electrical wire, although we really don't recommend this.

One of George's fields of study was that of electrical charge. As early as 1874, he introduced the term electrine but later revised it to electron as the fundamental unit

Physicist George J. Stoney (1826–1911).

quantity of electricity. His electron was only theoretical at the time, but his work contributed significantly to its discovery by J.J. Thomson six years later.

George coined the word by combining *electric* and *ion*, in case you're interested, and if you're not, here's a joke to finish with: An electron and a proton walk into a pub, and the proton says, 'It's your round'. The electron replies, 'Are you sure?' And the proton says, 'I'm positive.'

Epicentre, Seismology (noun)

(See Seismology)

Esker (noun)

Another geological term with which you may not be too familiar is esker, a long ridge of compacted sand or gravel separating two plains. And anyone who's driven the M6 between Dublin and Galway has probably seen Ireland's most famous esker, the Esker Riada, not paid it a blind bit of attention and gone back to singing along to (aka strangling) 'The Joker' by The Steve Miller Band, or if you're totally musically taste-free, some piece of oul' sentimental shite by Boyzone.

But back to matters in hand. An esker is formed in ice-walled tunnels within a glacier. Water flowing through them deposits material eroded by the glacier from the surrounding landscape over thousands of years. When the glaciers eventually melt away, hey presto, you're left with

Franz Josef Glacier, New Zealand.

a long, winding yoke that looks like a gigantic, meandering railway embankment.

There are thousands of eskers all over the world, and in the Arctic they actually often build roads directly on top of them. The world's longest is the Thelon Esker in Canada (800km or 500 miles) and the highest is Great Esker Park (27m, or 88ft) in Massachusetts.

The Esker Riada isn't continuous, thanks mainly to erosion or human activity, but in the Celtic world it was known as *An Slí Mór,* or 'The Great Highway', a kind of ancient M6. Esker Hills Golf Club in Offaly takes its name from the term, and if you look it up on Google Maps you can easily identify a long section of the Esker Riada cutting though the surrounding plains, which is no doubt speckled with lost golf balls from the club's more wojus golfers.

The term, by the way, comes from the Irish word *eiscir,* meaning ridge.

'FOUND THE BALL BUT LOST THE BLEEDIN' GOLF COURSE!'

Fail better (saying)

Among the most beloved of personal philosophies, or simply slogans, of sports stars, business tycoons, actors, writers, artists and so on, this famous phrase is an exhortation to persevere in the face of

IF AT FIRST YOU DON'T SUCCEED, YOU CAN EXPECT CRITICISM.

failure, to learn from the experience and the next time to fail better. Some of the above have even tattooed the line on their arms, legs and various other body parts for all we know. It's from a piece of prose called 'Worstward Ho' written by Samuel Beckett in 1983 and the full quote goes: 'Ever tried. Ever failed. No matter. Try again. Fail again. Fail better'.

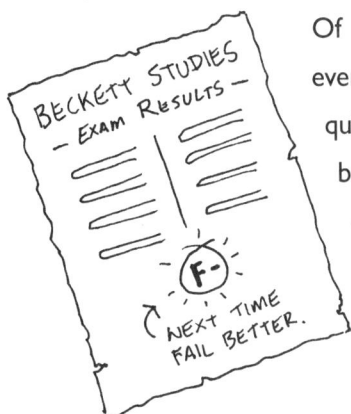

BECKETT STUDIES – EXAM RESULTS –

F-

NEXT TIME FAIL BETTER.

Of course, it's not the first line ever to encourage one never to quit. In fact, you can go all the way back to Robert the Bruce, King of Scotland, in 1314, who is said to have seen a spider making multiple attempts to weave a

Samuel Beckett (1906–1989).

web in a cave where he was hiding from the English, and subsequently encouraged his troops to 'Try, try, try again' until they were victorious. It worked anyway, as soon after they kicked the Sassenachs' arses at Bannockburn.

Of course, Beckett's line is *so* much cooler.

Galore

This one seems like it should have been obvious, at least to anyone who attended school in Ireland and had a *cúpla focal* battered into their little heads. You'll almost certainly have heard the phrase *ceart go leor*, which literally means 'right enough', the *go leor* bit leading us to the anglicised version: galore. The phrase originated in the seventeenth century and, as the years went by, the meaning evolved from merely 'enough' to 'in abundance'.

Something you probably haven't noticed or thought about is the fact

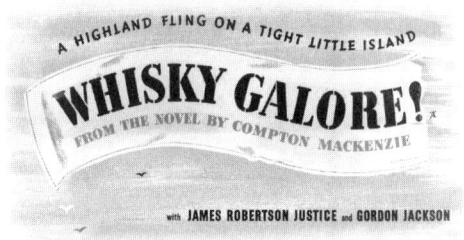

A HIGHLAND FLING ON A TIGHT LITTLE ISLAND

WHISKY GALORE!

FROM THE NOVEL BY COMPTON MACKENZIE

with JAMES ROBERTSON JUSTICE and GORDON JACKSON

that galore is a postpositive adjective i.e. an adjective that appears after the noun. And who would blame you for not thinking about that when you've other important things galore to think about? It's also unusual because, at different stages in its history, it has been defined as both a noun ('Jaysus, me poor head, I had a galore of drink') and an adverb ('Bleedin' hangovers, of course, I've had galore'), before it finally decided it was an adjective.

Galore's influence has reached far and wide. It has given itself to the names of businesses … eh … galore. There's BBQs Galore, Sandwiches Galore, Doors Galore and Knickers Galore – you name it. There's even a Girls Galore (not what you think!), which is a women's clothes shop. The word also gave its name to several movies, the most famous being the classic Ealing comedy *Whisky Galore!*, which was followed by a sequel *Rockets Galore!*, and a 2013 Australian romance *Galore*. The word was also the name of a 1997 album by The Cure, and finally and unforgettably, it was the surname of one of the most memorable 'Bond girls' – Pussy Galore. That one almost fell foul of US censors, but the producers somehow managed to persuade them that her first name referred to her cat-like abilities and if they thought otherwise then they were all dirty-minded oul' feckers.

And there you have it – useless information galore!

Garryowen (noun)

One for the rugby fans, most of whom will be familiar with the term describing an 'up and under' kick, which came into widespread use in the 1970s, thanks mainly to the commentaries of the encyclopaedic Scot, Bill McClaren.

Some detail for non-rugby people: a garryowen is when a player kicks the ball forward but with a very high arc, not gaining much distance but giving his teammates time to rush forward and tackle any would-be catcher. Imagine the guy waiting for the ball to descend, one eye skywards, the other on the six giant lumps of sweaty, mud-covered muscle hurtling towards him with murder in

their eyes. His jocks would need several runs through the washing machine, one would speculate.

Anyway, the term was coined after Garryowen Rugby Club in County Limerick used the tactic to great effect between 1924 and 1926, winning three Senior Cups. It was well known in Ireland in subsequent decades, but Bill McClaren introduced it to an international audience between 1953 and 2002, and thereafter the term became pretty much universal.

Get on one's nerves (saying)

In a 2004 speech in New York, Roddy Doyle had a real go at James Joyce, claiming his book *Ulysses* was 'overrated and overlong'. Here's a sample of what Doyle had to say: 'The whole idea that [Joyce] owns language as it is spoken in Dublin is a nonsense. He didn't invent the Dublin accent … it gets on my nerves.'

Whatever Roddy's view on Joyce, he probably was unaware that the phrase he used at the end of that sentence first appeared, certainly in written form, in the very book that he was slating. In fact, it appears four times:

IN YER FACE, DOYLER.

Chapter 11: Wish I hadn't promised to meet.
Freer in air. Music. Gets on your nerves.

Chapter 13: ... Gerty wished to goodness they
would take their squalling baby home out
of that and not get on her nerves ...

Chapter 18: I hate those rich shops get on your
nerves nothing kills me altogether only he thinks
he knows a great lot about a woman's dress and
... as I was washing myself there below with the glove
get on your nerves then doing the loglady all day ...

But most people would confess that *Ulysses*' endless pages of stream of consciousness and rambling interior monologue would eventually, well, get on your nerves.

Glen (noun)

Another geographical word that is universally used in English-speaking countries, 'glen' comes from the Irish/Scottish Celtic word *gleann* meaning mountain valley. Not much more to say about glen, except that it forms part of a ganseyload of Irish place names, it is the first name of an Irish Oscar winner for Best Original Song, there's a village

Glen of Imaal, County Wicklow.

in Donegal called Glen, and it's an acronym for the Gay and Lesbian Equality Network!

Gob (noun, verb) & Gobsmacked (adjective) & Gobstopper (noun)

Gob, meaning either a mouth or to spit forcefully (or to use the slang term, emit a gollier – that's a lump of phlegm that has been spat, for the uninitiated), originated from the old Irish word *gob,* meaning beak. It's a word that has given us such lovely and useful phrases as 'shut your f*****g gob' or 'I'll give ye a bleedin' box in the gob.'

Gobsmacked, meaning astonished or flabbergasted, is another English word owing its existence to the term, being a union of the words gob and smacked, i.e. a person is so shocked by some event that they look like they've been given the aforementioned box in the gob. And the gobstoppers that we all enjoyed and nearly choked to death on as kids also owe their name to the Celtic word for beak.

Gob has also made a significant contribution to the lexicon of Irish slang, forming part of gobdaw, which is defined as a person of limited mental capacity, usually depicted with his/her gob hanging open in a slack-jawed manner. And also, and perhaps more significantly, there's the tremendous word gobshite, which is almost worthy of a separate entry as it is slowly being adopted into the English language and is more and more frequently heard in British TV dramas, often spoken by non-Irish characters.

And you can't blame them for wanting it, can you? Gobshite is such a great word that just saying it aloud somehow warms the cockles of the heart. It can be applied to any number of people of either sex: useless politicians, crap sports people, your annoying next-door neighbour, the guy who cuts across your lane at 100km/h, the pharmacist who charges you €6.50 for a pack of aspirin.

In fact, it's so flexible and powerful an Irish insult that we really should apply for 'gobshite' to be given UNESCO world heritage status as a word of unique national and international cultural significance.

Hillbilly (noun)

The debate on this one is ongoing in American etymological circles, but there is a lot of evidence to support the idea that the often-derogatory term hillbilly, which was originally applied to residents of the Appalachian Mountains, had its origins in the language of Protestant Ulster Irish settlers.

Nowadays the term sort of means a country bumpkin or clodhopper and is definitely non-PC. But back in the day it was simply a name applied to early settlers from Ulster who were supporters of King William III, and who were also known as Billy Boys. And as the area in which they took up residence was high in the hills, well, put one and one together …

Although it should be said that, while the term hillbilly was probably around since the days of the first settlers, its earliest known appearance in print is in a 1900 *New York Journal* article, which had a very northern Yankee/city slicker bias, and describes the hillbilly thus: '… he lives in the hills, has no means to speak of, dresses as he

Hillbillies visiting Capitol Hill.

William III of England.

can, talks as he pleases, drinks whiskey when he gets it, and fires off his revolver as the fancy takes him'.

And it may be from prejudiced reports like this that hillbilly evolved into an offensive term. But one suspects the absolute true origin of the word may be lost forever in the Appalachian mists ...

Hollywood (noun, adj.)

The name has entered the English language as a generic term for the movies and the culture that surrounds them, and the area of Los Angeles that is the haunt of multimillionaire movie stars, directors and producers. In fact, it is arguably the most recognisable place name on the entire planet.

Yet few people outside County Wicklow, and especially in America, will realise that, in all likelihood, Hollywood takes its name from the tiny village of eighty people nestling in the Wicklow hills.

Back at the height of the Great Famine, the village of Hollywood was the residence of one Matthew Guirke, who, like about a million of us, decided that he didn't fancy the idea of starving to death, so he upped sticks and headed for the New World in 1850 at the age of twenty-four. Once there, he and his family led a somewhat

TINSELTOWN HERE
WE COME!!!

HOLLYWOOD ⇨
POPULATION 12

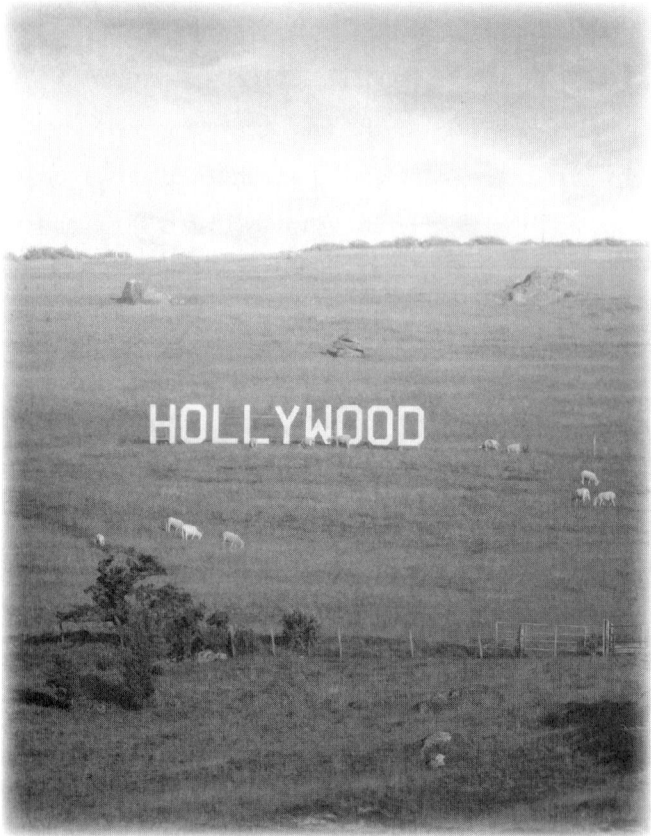

peripatetic existence, and among the places they lived were South Carolina, Nevada, Montana and, crucially, California. Skilled as a blacksmith and horse breeder, he did well for himself and had earned sufficient spondulicks to build a home *and* buy a racetrack in the state, which he named after his native Wicklow village: Hollywood.

The village decided to bring the story full circle in 2011, because just as Matthew had put the Hollywood in, well,

Hollywood, California, the locals put the Hollywood sign in Hollywood, Wicklow! They erected a slightly smaller yet impressive copy of the sign on the grassy hillside overlooking the village. It's worthy of a movie adaptation.

Hooligan (noun)

Here's how to recognise a modern hooligan. He (and it usually is a he) has a tight haircut or has gone full skinhead, the fact of which is often concealed by a hoodie, which sort of defeats the purpose of the hairdo in the first place, but then hooligans are, by and large, as thick as shite. In the past, very uncomfortable boots were the footwear of choice, as they were useful for kicking the bejaysus out of unsuspecting citizens, but nowadays expensive trainers (preferably stolen) are more acceptable. They'll often wear jeans, but wearing shorts in the middle of winter is also common as it demonstrates how tough they are, while allowing us to snigger at the fact that their goolies have most likely shrivelled to resemble a used teabag.

THAT'S WHAT YOU GET FOR CALLING ME A HOOLIGAN!

They have been known by a variety of terms during the last century or so, including lout, hoodlum, larrikin, skinhead, yobbo, yahoo (see Yahoo), hoodie, gobshites and so on, but 'hooligan' predates the lot. While it is definitely Irish in origin, there are a couple of possible sources. One dates from 1890s British music halls and a stereotype wild

Irish character called O'Hooligan. Shocking. It's so unlike the British to stereotype foreigners! The more likely source is from a gang of criminal youths in Lambeth, London, called 'The Hooligan Boys', led by one Patrick O'Hooligan, who were running wild in 1898. *The Daily Graphic* reported: '... the avalanche of brutality ... under the name of "Hooliganism" has cast such a dire slur on the social records of South London'.

After that the word came into widespread use in Britain and across the world, including Ireland. Little did Patrick know that he was giving his name to the English language, a name now meaning 'waste of space halfwit slimebucket'. He would have been *so* proud.

Hubbub (noun)

Not a word of a lie, but back in the sixteenth century, when our lads were preparing to charge into battle *en masse* and impale as many of the dirty, heathen, invading Sassenachs on their pikes as possible, the war cry would go up: *Ub! Ub! Ub!* which was an expression of utter contempt akin to 'ye manky bleedin' shower of shite hawks!'

... AND ABOVE ALL, LADS,
GO OUT THERE AND
ENJOY YERSELVES.

And with several hundred screaming, bloodthirsty voices overlapping it would have sounded like *ubububububub* to the unfortunate English intruders.

So, those who survived and returned to England with their heads still attached to their shoulders, although possibly missing several other bodily parts, began to describe the chaotic, frenzied din to their compatriots as a terrible *ububub*, which eventually morphed into hubbub as the centuries passed.

Irish Coffee (noun)

Isn't it strange that the two drinks for which Ireland is most famous look almost identical to each other except for the fact that one is the size of a pint and the other is pint-sized?

But it's probably a coincidence that the inventor contrived to create a drink that essentially looks like Guinness in a wine glass!

Intentional or not, you can visit a restaurant or bar in places as far flung as Mongolia, Panama or Indonesia and the staff might be limited to their native tongue, yet they'll still understand the term Irish coffee.

The famed cocktail was first created in 1947 by head chef Joe Sheridan in the terminal at Foynes, County Limerick, which was a key stopping point for transatlantic seaplanes in the 1930s and '40s. The story goes that a bunch of American tourists had just arrived, knackered and as cold as an Eskimo's arse after their journey in the draughty plane, when Joe came to the rescue with his concoction of Irish whiskey, sugar and hot, black coffee, blended and topped by carefully poured cream (note: whipped cream does not qualify, and neither does using Scotch whisky). Well, the soon semi-rat-arsed Americans were knocking them back faster than Joe could produce them.

Word took off faster than a seaplane and in 1952 a renowned American travel writer, Stanton Delaplane, (yes, Delaplane, really!) introduced Irish coffee to the wider world. He first persuaded the owner of San Francisco's

famed Buena Vista Café to serve the drink, and the pair spent so long mastering the art of pouring the cream and testing the results that Delaplane collapsed gee-eyed on the tram tracks outside. Honest!

After that, the drink began to spread to the four points of the compass, and by the mid-1960s it was pretty much universal.

Last word to movie star and comedian Danny Kaye, who in 1957 said of Irish coffee: 'There's nothing funny about this drink, it's nectar!'

Jack-o'-lantern (noun)

What the feck is a Jack-o'-lantern, we hear some of you ask. Well, you'll probably be more familiar with this yoke as a Halloween decoration of a carved-out pumpkin with a candle inside. It's ironic that sometimes you hear people decry American culture's non-stop trampling of Irish tradition, such as with the pumpkin thing, when in fact – in this case – it's the other way around: we actually gave the Jack-o'-lantern to the Yanks only for them to give it back.

You've also probably never heard of Stingy Jack. Well, this is a very old Irish myth with many variations in the telling, but essentially boils down to this lad Jack double-crossing the Devil in a deal, which ensured his soul was ever after condemned to wander the bogs of Ireland with only a hollowed-out turnip and candle to guide his way. To keep Jack's spirit away, Irish people then began to carve turnips with scary faces, displaying them in windows in the hope of scaring the shite out of the mischievous Jack, which seems a tad optimistic, given that Jack had already had dealings with Satan himself.

WELL, SPEAK OF THE DEVIL.

Irish immigrants brought this tradition to the US where, the Americans being, well, American, decided to take the idea but make it much bigger, and began using pumpkins instead of turnips, the bigger the better. A tradition with genuine roots. Haha.

Keening (verb)

This used to be practised as the norm at Irish funerals up to the early twentieth century, but gradually faded into silence, thanks be to Jaysus, as it would have driven most people to an early grave.

The term itself is an anglicisation of the old Irish word *caoineadh* meaning to weep, and involved a keener, usually a woman, 'singing' a lament over the body of the deceased. The keener was usually professional and often hadn't a clue as to the identity of the stiff, but was provided with a resumé of his/her human qualities and great deeds in life, etc. The keen itself was built around a very basic melody, which would be repeated *ad infinitum* and could be shortened or lengthened to suit the listing of the corpse's character references. There was no rhythm or rhyme, and words could be interspersed with long wails. So basically, it must have sounded like a bag of live cats being slowly dissolved in a vat of sulphuric acid.

The practice may have gone the way of the dodo, but so unpleasant was it on the ears that the term has entered the English language as a word meaning shrill or screeching. A dentist's drill could be described as having a keening sound. Not that such information will be much

I'M SO SORRY. NEVER MET
WERE YOU CLOSE? THE GUY.

use as the spinning bit begins to grind holes in your pearly whites!

Kelvin Scale (noun)

There's an old joke among scientists about a researcher who announces that he's going to freeze himself to −273.15 degrees. His friends tell him he's nuts, but he reassures them that he'll be OK. That's 0 Kelvin, geddit? Well, it's probably not that funny to non-thermodynamic students, among which, treasured reader, we assume you are numbered.

Like the old song 'you say "tomato", I say "tomayto" …' when it comes to temperature measurement, Europeans say Celsius, Americans say Fahrenheit and scientists/engineers say Kelvin.

LADIES & GENTLEMEN… I GIVE YOU ABSOLUTE ZERO!

THANKS FOR NOTHING!

William Thomson, 1st Baron Kelvin (1824–1907).

The Kelvin Scale takes its name from Lord Kelvin, aka William Thomson, who was born in Belfast in 1824, worked for most of his career in Scotland and was one of the most renowned boffins of his day. He is best known nowadays for inventing the international system of absolute temperature. He did sterling work in the fields of thermodynamics, electricity, geophysics, magnetism and telegraphy and played a key role in the laying of the first transatlantic telegraph cable from Valentia Island, County Kerry to Newfoundland, Canada.

In 1892 he was appointed to the House of Lords, and became Lord Kelvin, though even the name 'Kelvin' has Irish origins, from *caol* meaning narrow and *abhainn* meaning river.

Kelvin was the first to determine that absolute zero was reached at −273.15 degrees Celsius, and he set this point as 0 on his new scale. However, there are no degrees in the Kelvin Scale, just kelvins − clearly his lordship was determined that scientists would never forget his name.

Now that you know all that, go back and reread the joke.

Geddit?

Kibosh (noun)

Although it sort of sounds like a Jewish festival or something you might order in a Middle Eastern restaurant ('can I have the kibosh with dumplings, please?') that's probably coincidental and, although not conclusive, the odds suggest that both the word 'kibosh' and the phrase 'put the kibosh on' have Irish origins. We're claiming it anyway.

A version of it first appeared in print in no less a work than Charles Dickens' *Sketches by Boz* when a character

IS IT JUST ME OR
DO YOU LOOK YOUNGER
WITHOUT THE HOOD?

exclaims 'Hoo-roar, put the kye-bosk on her, Mary.' This scene was set in Seven Dials near Covent Garden, London, a poverty-stricken area with a very high Irish population.

Putting the kibosh on, meaning 'putting a stop to something' or 'dispose of something definitively', likely originates from the Irish term *caip bháis*, which means death cap and was said to be the black cap a judge donned before sentencing some poor fecker to the gallows, which is definitely disposing of something definitively. Alternatively, *caip bháis* referred to a covering pulled over the face of a corpse before burial, sort of putting the kibosh on the dead guy's life.

Other theories include the French verb *cabocher* meaning 'cut the head off', or a hot iron bar used to soften leather, and called a kibosh, used by clogmakers, but that term appeared only in 1860, thirty years after it appeared in Dickens, so it's possible that it took its name from the original meaning.

So we'd like to officially put the kibosh on any alternative origins. We're claiming kibosh as one of our own!

Leprechaun (noun)

Well, nobody is going to dispute that this is an Irish term. The leprechaun is pretty universally recognised as a magical little man who keeps a pot of gold at the end of a rainbow. The word itself comes from the old Irish *lupracán*, meaning small body, but the modern depiction of the leprechaun with a green jacket and top hat sitting on a toadstool is basically a load of oul' Oirish b****x.

Traditionally, leprechauns had red coats with gold embroidery, either cone-shaped or cocked hats (like Napoleon's), white breeches and they definitely never sat on toadstools or any other type of fungus, which was probably borrowed from European folk tales. Like the modern image of Santa Claus, which was essentially created by Coca Cola, the modern leprechaun

AT THE END OF THE RAINBOW YOU'LL FIND A LITTLE POT.

A touch O'Blarney... a heap O'Magic and
A LOAD O'LAUGHTER!

WALT DISNEY'S
Darby O'Gill and
the Little People

was an invention of marketing eejits, all of whom threw in bits that they thought made him appear Oirish and mischievous.

Hollywood has made its own contribution to the leprechaun's image, giving us no fewer than eight of its *Leprechaun* slasher movie series, with the aforementioned sprite becoming more demonic as they progress. We also had the slightly less throat-slashing leprechaun in Disney's *Darby O'Gill and the Little People* (1959), while Nobel

Prize-winning economist Paul Krugman coined the term 'leprechaun economics' in response to the Irish Central Statistics Office's wonky GNP figures.

Of course, there is one genuine connection between leprechauns and fungi: consuming magic mushrooms is probably the only way you'll ever see one.

Life of Reilly (saying)

A much-used phrase in the English-speaking world, it describes someone living a carefree, fun-filled life of comfort and relaxation, rarely doing a tap of work, much like anyone in the Irish civil service.

Although undoubtedly having Irish connections, the phrase first appeared in a New Jersey newspaper in 1910, when it reported that 'Henry Mungersdorf is living the life of Riley just at present'. Who exactly Mr

TOM REILLY
1971 ~ 2024
HAD THE LIFE
OF REILLY UNTIL
HIS WIFE FOUND
OUT HE WAS
HAVING THE LIFE
OF REILLY.

GEORGE SIDNEY
& CHARLIE MURRAY

The LIFE of RILEY

Mungersdorf was is anyone's guess, but he has gained a small measure of immortality thanks to his association with the phrase. Note that there are no quotes around 'life of Riley', suggesting the phrase was already in popular use.

One plausible source is the 1855 Irish song 'Colleen Bawn', which is a story about one Willy Reilly eloping with a beautiful young heiress only to be caught and tried for kidnapping, but who is cleared because she reveals she went with him willingly, and eventually they live happily ever after, enjoying her old man's riches. One verse goes so:

Oh, my lord, he stole from her, her
    diamonds and her rings,

Gold watch and silver buckles and
    many precious things,
Which cost me in bright guineas more
    than five hundred pounds,
I'll have the life of Reilly, should I
    lose ten thousand pounds.

Another possible source is a popular song by George Gaskin, aka The Silver-Voiced Irish Tenor, who released 'The Best in the House is None Too Good for Reilly' in 1897, which includes the lines:

He's money for to pay,
So they let him have his way,
The best in the house is none too good for Reilly.

By the way, surviving recordings of George's 'silver voice' suggest that it could be reproduced by mixing the following sounds: Meg Ryan's fake orgasm in *When Harry met Sally*, rusty door hinges, squealing bicycle brakes and scratching nails on a blackboard.

Lilliputian (adj.)

The term, meaning very small or minuscule, made its first appearance in the English language in Jonathan Swift's *Gulliver's Travels* (1726) and within a few years it was in widespread use. It refers to the tiny inhabitants of the imaginary land of Lilliput, where he is shipwrecked. Gulliver describes how the Lilliputian emperor decreed that he be supplied with enough food and drink 'sufficient to support 1,724 Lilliputians', giving us some idea as to their scale. The number may have been inspired by the year in which he wrote that passage.

THE KIDS GROW SO QUICKLY THESE DAYS.

Swift's Lilliput was based on Nure, a real townland on the shores of Lough Ennell in County Westmeath. He was reputedly in a boat on the lough when he looked back at the shore and saw how small the people appeared. This inspired his fictional land of tiny folk, and eventually the townland was renamed Lilliput in his honour.

Jonathan Swift (1667–1745).

In terms of usage, consider the odds of Metro North being completed on time and in budget. Lilliputian.

Limerick (noun)

The most likely origin of this form of humorous, farcical

poetry is from the so-called Maigue Poets, a circle of eighteenth-century Gaelic poets in – where else – Limerick. And the term may also be linked to an early nonsense parlour game where one of the participants would say 'Will you or won't you come up to Limerick?' But there's really no doubt that the county gave its name to the English language in the form of witty five-line rhymes, of which there now exist roughly a gazillion. The early efforts were very polite, such as this from 1880:

There was a young rustic named Mallory,
Who drew but a very small salary,
When he went to the show,
His purse made him go
To a seat in the uppermost gallery.

As the decades advanced, some became slightly more risqué:

WHAT RHYMES WITH 'PAIN IN THE ARSE HUSBAND'?

There was a young lady named Alice,

Who was known to have peed in a chalice,

'Twas the common belief

It was done for relief,

And not out of Protestant malice.

And of course things progressed:

On the boob of a woman named Gail,

Was tattooed the price of her tail,

And on her behind,

For the sake of the blind,

Was the same information in braille.

We could go on … but we'll spare your blushes.

Lough (noun)

The term for a lake originates from the Irish word *loch*, which itself comes from the ancient Celtic word *loku* meaning pool.

Ireland is home to an amazing 12,000 loughs covering an area of about 1,200 km^2 (463 sq. miles), and that's just in the Republic. England's lakes, by contrast, cover a mere 320 km^2 (123 sq. miles).

The largest lough on the island is Lough Neagh at almost 400 km^2 (152 sq. miles) and reputedly the only lough in Ireland or Britain that extends beyond the horizon line. The deepest lough is Muckross near Killarney, at 75m (246ft).

According to folklore, beneath the glistening waters of

HONESTLY, THE HOOK WAS 'THIS' BIG!

Lough Neagh, County Antrim.

Killarney's Lough Leane lies the land of Tír na nÓg, the land of youth. Of course, the only way to verify this is to go there and drown yourself.

Lynch (verb)

This is one we would probably rather not trace back to Irish roots, but the practice of hanging carried out by a mob unfortunately comes from the Irish name that is common in Galway.

The name itself comes from the Irish word *loinseach*, variously meaning shipping/pirate/fleet, depending on where you look, but you get the idea that it has nautical associations.

One proposed origin, probably false, is that in 1674, the Mayor of Galway, one James Lynch fitz Stephen, sentenced his son to death for murdering a stranger and personally hanged him from his own house. But that's a judicial killing, approved in law, and not really a lynching.

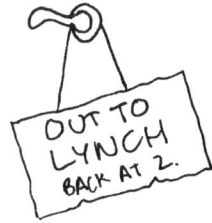

Much more likely is that the term originated from another man, called Charles Lynch, an Irish American military officer and judge in the American Revolutionary War. Lynch was born in Virginia in 1736, a decade after his father had emigrated from Ireland. After the war started in 1775, Lynch used his military position to carry out summary hangings of anyone still loyal to the British crown. Lynching, as it became known, was eventually practised, without trial, against people suspected of being criminals, and later against African Americans in the southern states during the American Civil War, during which thousands were murdered. Incredibly, this by now racist practice continued in places up to the 1940s.

One of the less pleasant words we gifted the English language.

Malapropism (noun)

With all the taxes from multinationals, Ireland has become a preposterous country, although in some years our tax collecting has been somewhat erotic, and many politicians are also putrefied that if corporate tax increases, the multinationals will show their dysentery by leaving. The government is not inflammable, and mistakes could be made, leaving Ireland an industrial dessert.

No, this book has not suddenly turned into an economic commentary, but the previous paragraph serves to demonstrate the meaning of the term 'malapropism' (there were six for you to spot!), when an incorrect word is used in place of a similar-sounding word. The term was created by the Irish playwright Richard Brinsley Sheridan

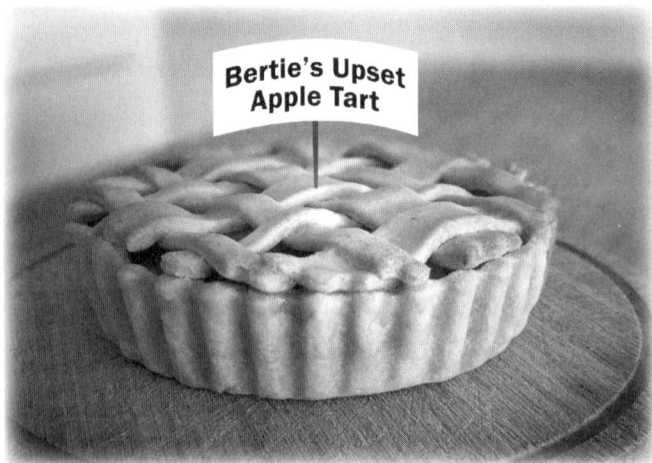

Bertie's Upset Apple Tart

when he introduced the world to the character of Mrs Malaprop in his 1775 play *The Rivals*. Mrs Malaprop's name is a union of the French word *mal* meaning bad and *apropos* meaning concerning, and she is famous for misusing words to humorous effect, such as: '… he is the very pineapple [pinnacle] of politeness', 'Illiterate [obliterate] him quite from your memory', and 'He's as headstrong as an allegory [alligator] on the banks of the Nile.'

Among some real-life malapropisms from the rich and famous are: 'Don't upset the apple tart' (Bertie Ahern), 'I might just fade into Bolivian' (Mike Tyson), and 'Now we have Nancy Pelosi's Gazpacho Police spying on Congress' (Marjorie Taylor Greene).

And we'll leave the last malapropism to former Aussie Prime Minister Tony Abbott, who memorably said, 'No one is the suppository of all wisdom …'.

Malarkey (noun)

Similar in meaning to blarney, except that it probably means more blatant lies, malarkey started life in print in the US, appearing in a cartoon strip by a famous cartoonist called Tad Dorgan, but it's possible it was in general use in America before that.

Although the term sounds Irish and is definitely an Irish surname, nobody really knows how it came to have the

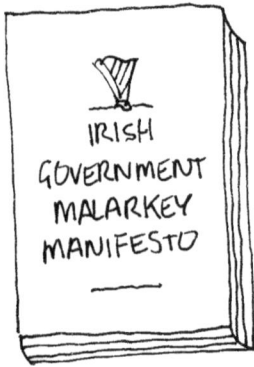

IRISH
GOVERNMENT
MALARKEY
MANIFESTO

current meaning, so it is possible that some long-dead Irish man or woman had a reputation as a complete bullshitter, and their name became associated with blatant fibbing, but no record has been found to confirm this.

One other suggestion is that it came from the Greek word *malakós* meaning soft/mild-mannered or another Greek word, *malakia*, meaning masturbation. But both of those seem a very long way from the accepted meaning of malarkey (especially the latter!). So that theory sounds like a load of, well, malarkey.

One other Irish origin theory is the old Irish word *mullachán*, which meant ruffian or strongly built boy. But that also sounds like a stretch.

US President Joe Biden has no doubts, having used the term countless times in his career. Referring to the word 'bullshit' in 2012 (without actually using that word), he said, 'We Irish call it malarkey.'

Modernism (noun)

Another Swiftian contribution, this one, and there are more to come. It is first recorded in the English language in a letter from Jonathan Swift to his fellow satirist Alexander Pope in 1737. It means deviating from classical and traditional styles, and clearly he wasn't a big fan of those who practised the term he'd just created, complaining: 'I wish you would give orders against the corruption of English by those scribblers who send us over to Ireland their

MODERNISM IS SO LAST YEAR.

trash in prose and verse, with abominable curtailings and quaint modernisms.'

Since then, the term has been used in the fields of literature, art, dance, architecture, philosophy and so on. But let's finish with some modernist humour.

'Say what you want about the deaf ...'. (Jimmy Carr)

'Working at the job centre has to be a tense job: knowing that if you get fired, you still have to come in the next day.' (Adam Rowe)

'Hedgehogs – why can't they just share the hedge?' (Dan Antopolski)

'My dad has suggested that I register for a donor card. He's a man after my own heart.' (Masai Graham)

'Say what you like about waiters, but I think they bring a lot to the table.' (Gary Delaney)

Moniker (noun)

The term, which means essentially nickname, finds its roots in the Irish Traveller language Shelta, and is a derivation of the word *mŭnnik,* meaning name. It was first recorded in the 1850s.

And it's appropriate that moniker is an Irish word, as we are masters at applying monikers to our fellow citizens, among other things. Dubliners have appended monikers to most of the statues in the city:

Molly Malone: The Tart with the Cart
James Joyce: The Prick with the Stick
Oscar Wilde: The Quare in the Square
Anna Livia: The Floozie in the Jacuzzi
Patrick Kavanagh: The Crank on the Bank
The Lady Shoppers: The Hags with the Bags
The Spire: The Stiletto in the Ghetto

And of course there's the long-lived moniker for the south-side suburb of Stillorgan – Mickey Marbh (in Irish *marbh*

SO WHY DO THEY CALL YOU PIPSQUEAK?

means dead or still). Among the wittier personal monikers that Irish people have bestowed on their fellow citizens are:

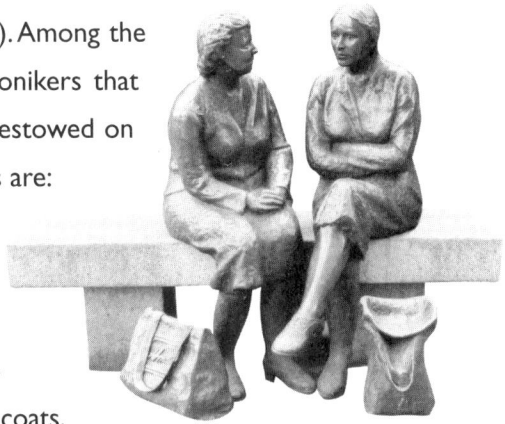

The guy called Dulux, because he never went anywhere without two coats.

The chap named Enda May, who was known as June.

Boomerang, who moved to Australia and came home a month later.

The fellow, who was engaged multiple times, called Lord of the Rings.

The man called Bungalow because there wasn't much up top but supposedly he was well furnished downstairs.

The girl called Kracow whose real name was Dawn.

The lad named Justin French, who was known as Garçon.

The taxi driver named Abdul, who was known affectionately as Abdul Abhaile.

And finally, the prize goes to the Gaelic footballer known as Chilli. Why? Because he was the son of Con Kearney.

Moonlighting (verb)

Commonly used as a term to mean that someone has taken a second job, unbeknownst to their employer – but the earliest known use of the term probably had absolutely nothing to do with work.

NO, THAT'S 'MOONING', MISTER McKEON.

Back in the Ireland of 1882 the Land War was in full swing (see also Boycott), with tenants refusing to pay rent to their landlords, and frequent evictions. Secret groups, known variously as Ribbonmen, Whiteboys or Threshers, began conducting a campaign of intimidation against landlords and those tenants who continued to pay rent. It was often violent and was condemned by Parnell's Land League, and could involve assault, or assassination in extreme cases. However, most of these yobbos were content with going out at night and performing such heroic acts as hamstringing cattle and horses, driving sheep over cliffs, burning crops, tearing down fencing and so on. The practice was known as moonlighting, and luckily it evolved to mean something slightly different as the decades advanced.

A meeting of Ribbonmen.

Orrery (noun)

What in the name of Jaysus is an orrery, we hear you ask. Isn't that some kind of bird enclosure? Nope, an orrery is a mechanical model of the solar system, and you've probably seen one or two in museums or in movies.

They're actually amazing things, intricately interlinking wheels and cogs that replicate the spin of the planets and their respective orbits of the sun – although not usually to scale, because if you represented Mercury as pea-sized, the sphere representing the sun would be roughly the size of a hot-air balloon. That would make your orrery a tad difficult to display on the mantelpiece.

The first mechanical orrery of the modern scientific

era was made by English clockmaker George Graham in 1710, and a copy was made as a gift for his patron, Charles Boyle. Boyle was not only a member of the Irish Parliament for Charleville in Cork at the time, but also the 4th Earl of Orrery, a barony in County Cork, so the device ended up taking the title.

Pet (noun, verb)

A bit hazy this one, mists of time and all that, but there is a good possibility that 'pet' is derived from the Irish word *petta*. Of course there's also a possibility that it comes from its near relative in Scots Gaelic *peata*,

BE A PET
AND BRING
ME WALKING!

TEACHER'S PET

or possibly from a bit of both. According to the *Oxford English Dictionary* (OED), there was also another, earlier word 'pet' that was completely separate from Gaelic and derived from the Latin *pedere* meaning the act of breaking wind. A fart, but let's put that behind us.

While 'pet' is usually a term for your beloved shih-tzu whom you have amusingly named Groucho Barks, or your cockatoo whom you've taught to say 'Go an' ask me bollix', it has also become a term of affection (or condescension in certain cases), and the name applied to the teacher's favourite pupil, who was always some smart-arsed little bastard. And for your interest, it is also the acronym used for Positron Electron Tomography, not to mention the plastic polyethylene terephthalate, but we draw the line at claiming they have an ancient Celtic origin.

Phoney (adj.)

In J.D. Salinger's *The Catcher in the Rye*, Holden Caulfield famously describes everything he dislikes as phony (US spelling), while ignoring the fact that he himself frequently acted in a phoney manner. What the mixed-up teen probably didn't know, or care to know for that matter, as he was a fairly self-centred little shite, was that the descriptor he loved so much could trace its roots back to Ireland and is an Irish word still in use today.

Back in the eighteenth and nineteenth centuries, there existed a confidence trick in England run by Fawney men and known as the Fawney Rig. This involved dropping a ring in the street that appeared to be solid gold but was

I'M TALKING TO YOUR DEAD FATHER. HE SAYS HIS NAME IS BOB? ...TOM? ... NO, WAIT... JAMES?... VINCENT?... CORMAC?... MAYBE, COLM?

in fact merely brass with a thin gilt. When a passer-by saw it, thinking he'd struck lucky, the cute hoor Fawney man would leap forward and claim he'd spotted the ring first. A negotiation was then carried out, with the Fawney man agreeing eventually to settle with the other for an agreed price, the poor sucker thinking he'd still got a great bargain, only to discover at the jewellers that he'd been had.

So what's all this got to do with Ireland? Well, fawney itself derives from the Irish word *fáinne,* meaning ring, taking us full circle back to 'phoney'.

Puck (name)

This is the name of a key character in Shakespeare's *A Midsummer Night's Dream.* Puck, the 'merry wanderer of the night', who is a mischievous fairy or sprite, probably takes his name from one of several related and similar-sounding words in the Celtic languages, including the Irish word *púca,* meaning spirit or ghost. It's probably no coincidence either that both Puck and the Irish *púca* are both shape-shifting entities.

Shakespeare includes references to Ireland/Irish more than forty times in his works, not to mention other Celtic nations, so is very likely to have come across many an Irish term in his research. Scholars actually think that the

Bard's original version of Macbeth's soliloquy went thus:

Is this a dagger I see before me?

The handle toward my hand?

It is in me bollix.

Puck (noun)

This puck is the yoke that ice hockey players batter around the rink, and it has its origins in the Irish word *poc*.

Most Irish people will probably be familiar with the *Poc Fada* contest, where players compete to see who can wallop the *sliotar* the furthest – the phrase literally means 'long puck'. The term most likely entered America via the Irish settlers in Nova Scotia, where they continued to practise their traditional age-old Irish pastimes of playing hurling and then getting fluthered drunk afterwards.

The most wins ever in the *Poc Fada* championships, incidentally, is by Brendan Cummins from Tipperary, with nine victories. You have to hand it to him: it's some pucking achievement.

OH PUCK!

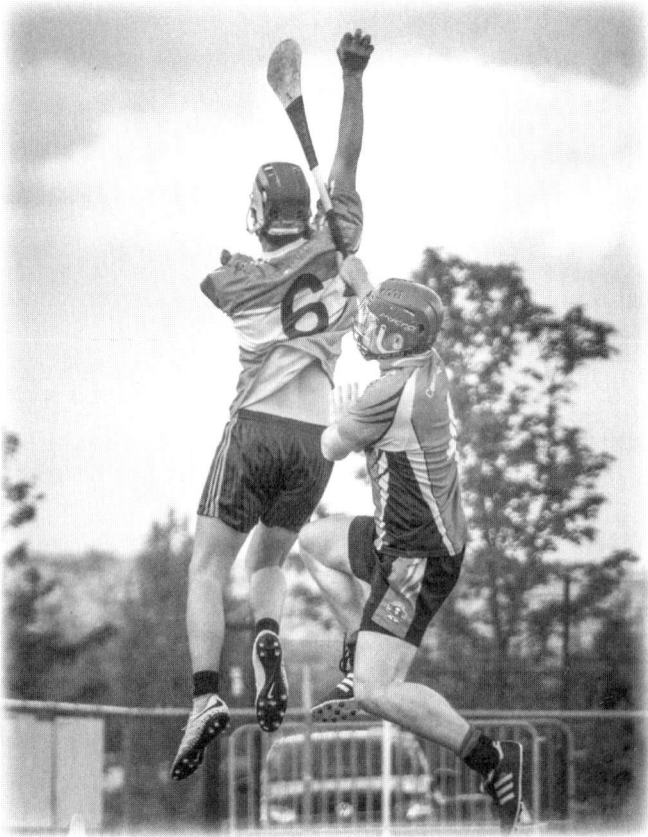

Puss, Sourpuss (noun)

If any yobbo ever says to you 'D'ye want a bleedin' slap in the puss?' one response might be to distract him by explaining the origin of the term puss, meaning face. Calmly inform him that the word is completely unrelated to the term for cat, but in fact has its roots in an Irish word for snout, which is *pus*.

The same Irish word can also mean mouth but this is when it is used in contempt, as 'Shut your big ugly *pus*'. Actually, it is more likely that said yobbo is using it in this context, as considering the fact that he is threatening to slap you in the first place, one would assume that it's not out of affection.

You might also inform him that the term was most likely popularised outside Ireland by emigrants to the US, among whom pugilism was a highly popular sport, and where it was used frequently by boxing coaches when advising their man on the optimal target to aim for.

The Americans also appended our puss with the adjective sour to produce 'sourpuss', meaning someone with an expression that looks like they have half a lemon in their gob.

TAKE THAT PUSS
OFF YOUR FACE —
RIGHT NOW!

Which brings us back to your yobbo. Now, while he's thinking about all that, run like feck.

Put to the pin of your collar (saying)

While it definitely has Irish origins, how precisely it came to mean what it does is a bit more inconclusive. It means to be forced to make a big effort or to be put in a very difficult position.

Back in the day, shirts came with separate collars, which seems a bit nuts nowadays, but actually had a very practical purpose. Laundering clothes was difficult, thanks to a lack of running water. It was also time-consuming and an extra expense. So, in 1827, a woman called Hannah Montague invented the detachable collar, which was much simpler to clean in isolation and allowed her husband to present the appearance of having a clean shirt every day, although you have to imagine that the guy must have smelled like a jockey's bollox after a while in the same shirt. Anyway, the fashion took and spread rapidly.

The collar was attached to the shirt by a pin, which brings us to the explanation for the saying as it developed in Ireland. In the nineteenth century, pins were also required for other parts of male clothing, such as cuffs, and even to attach a waistcoat to a thing called a trousers band, which was a narrow piece of material sewn onto the waist of trousers. The pin for this essentially prevented his trousers from falling down, so if there was a shortage of pins, the poor man had to resort to using the collar pin to save his modesty. He was put to the pin of his collar.

Thank Christ for jeans and T-shirts.

Quark (noun)

No, it's not a vegetarian meat substitute (that's Quorn) and the fact is that you wouldn't exist without quarks. Nor would anything else, for that matter.

There's an old joke you probably heard in secondary school that went: 'Never trust an atom. They make up everything.' And that is very true, and you probably also remember from science lessons that every atom contains a nucleus with electrons buzzing around it. The nucleus is made up of protons and neutrons (which are giants compared to the electron). Electrons are negative, protons are positive and neutrons are neutral, much like Ireland or Switzerland. Atoms are really, really, really small, and protons are even smaller; 84 million billion of them lined up side by side would measure just one metre (3ft).

But in the 1960s Nobel Prize-winning physicist Murray Gell-Mann predicted the existence of an even smaller little bowsie: the quark. Quarks are indivisible and have different 'flavours' – that's what physicists call them, being the witty types that they are. And to demonstrate how even wittier they are, they named the flavours up, down, charm, strange, top and bottom. Now, when you've stopped rolling around laughing at such comedic brilliance, we'll continue. The latter four only exist during high-energy collisions, and we're not talking about someone rear-ending your car. Think particle accelerators. So we only have to concern ourselves with the up and down quarks. Every proton has two ups and one down, and every neutron has two downs and one up, which is starting to sound like a game of snakes and ladders. And that's really all you need to know

Physicist Murray Gell-Mann (1929–2019).

about quarks. Except, of course, for why you're reading this. Well, when Murray Gell-Mann first conceived of them, he had a vague sound in his head to describe them, which was 'kwork'. But the physicist also liked to dip into James Joyce's *Finnegans Wake* for some light reading every now and then, and there he came across the line 'Three quarks for Muster Mark!'

And so he named the new particle.

Now as protons and neutrons are made up of quarks and as we also contributed the word electron to the world, it essentially means that Ireland has supplied the names for all the matter in the universe!

Physicists also have a particle called a God Particle, by the way. Maybe they'll rename it the Jaysus Particle.

Ruction (noun)

An example of another word that originated in Ireland (very probably) but not in the Irish language. There is general agreement that ruction, meaning a noisy disturbance or uproar, began its life in the wake of the 1798 Rebellion, when we had the temerity to rise up against the British because they were brutalising, impoverishing, intimidating and imprisoning us. The cheek of us!

Things aren't exactly clear how the word emerged from the chaos of the battlefield, but it is generally thought that it was a shortening of another term such as insurrection

THERE WAS A FIERCE RUCTION IN THE DÁIL WHEN SOMEONE SUGGESTED SHUTTING THE BAR EARLY.

or destruction. How exactly that happened is unknown, just that the earliest use of the word specifically made reference to the rebellion.

Ruction, when later combined with rumpus, also gave us another word with a similar meaning, ruckus. Two for the price of one.

To get back to 1798, and the reason the Irish were rebelling?

The British were revolting.

Sassenach (noun, adj.)

We had to put up with the filthy Sassenachs' bloodthirsty marauding and misrule for 750 years, so it's not surprising that someone came up with a somewhat derogatory term or two for them. Of course, we have also developed many other unflattering terms for the former invaders of these shores, but most of those are unprintable, and besides, there aren't enough pages in this book to fit them all.

The origin of the word is from the Irish Gaelic *Sasanach*, the Scots Gaelic *Sasunnoch* and the Welsh *Seisnig*, and they're all rooted in the old term for the English: Saxons. When the word made an appearance in Joyce's *Ulysses*, it brought the word to a truly international audience: '... the Sassenach tried to starve the nation at home while the land was full of crops that the British hyenas bought and sold ...' (Episode 12, Cyclops).

We share the origins of Sassenach with our Scottish and Welsh cousins, who also had cause to view their English neighbours with something less than admiration. (They really pissed everyone off, didn't they?) Anyway, we're all friends now, and the term is usually employed in a sort of mildly disparaging manner, as in 'the Sassenach eejits actually voted for Brexit, haha.'

Seismology, Epicentre (noun)

The bombing campaign unleashed by a little-known Irishman in Killiney and Dalkey in Dublin, and in Wales, using tons of high explosives, doesn't get much mention in the history books recording our turbulent history of conflict. And the reason for that is because it had absolutely nothing to do with politics, but was

Seismologist Robert Mallet (1810–1881).

THIS SHOULD SHAKE THINGS UP A BIT.

scientific in nature. It was carried out by a man who should, by all accounts, have a statue somewhere in Ireland in his honour, but sadly is virtually unknown by most Irish people. His name was Robert Mallet (1810–1881) and he was an internationally renowned geophysicist and civil engineer who is regarded as the 'Father of Seismology'. He carried out pioneering work in earthquake research first in Ireland, then in Wales and finally in Italy, which led to a ground-breaking (sorry!) paper: *The Great Neapolitan Earthquake of 1857: The First Principles of Observational Seismology.*

But back to Killiney, or the beach to be specific: Mallet decided to bury a bunch of 12kg (26lb) bombs a couple of metres down in the sand, detonate them and record the effect over a kilometre (0.6 miles) away. The shock waves were almost certainly felt by the well-to-do populace, and undoubtedly many a brandy was rippled and cup of tea toppled from the startled fingers of those Victorian ladies.

He then repeated the experiments on Dalkey Island and observed that the waves travelled twice as fast through the rock as they had through the sand of the beach. And when a devastating earthquake struck Italy's Basilicata region in 1857, killing between eleven thousand and nineteen thousand people, he was commissioned to travel there and continue his work, which he did with great success, employing photography as a pioneering tool to record the devastation.

Robert took the ancient Greek word *seismos* (to shake) and added *logy* (the study of) and gave the world the term seismology. He also took another Greek word *epikentros* (upon the centre) and coined the word epicentre, which is the point on Earth's surface directly above the point where the earthquake originated in Earth's crust. Of course, epicentre has taken on a wider meaning beyond geology, e.g. 'Temple Bar in Dublin is the epicentre of rip-off Ireland …'.

Shamrock (noun)

This is so associated with Ireland you'd be sort of gob-smacked if we hadn't been responsible for coining the term for this particular type of clover, whose official name in botanical circles is either *Trifolium repens* or *Trifolium dubium*. However, going into a shop and asking 'Can I have a bunch of *Trifolium dubium*, please?' might get you a smack in the gob, so we'll stick with the term that is known the world over.

It comes from the Irish word *seamróg* and, as you almost certainly know but we'll tell you anyway, legend has it that St Patrick used the shamrock with its three leaves to explain the concept of the Holy Trinity to his converts.

In the eighteenth century, revolutionary groups such as the United Irishmen began to use the shamrock as a symbol for Ireland and by the nineteenth century it had become inextricably linked with all things Irish. Thomas Moore even wrote a poem in its praise:

The green immortal Shamrock!
Chosen leaf
Of Bard and Chief,
Old Erin's native Shamrock!

And in the last fifty years it has been elevated to gloried status in the form of the inflatable plastic shamrock, shamrock head boppers and shamrock-shaped sunglasses; the ladies can even get a shamrock-shaped bra and the boys shamrock-shaped jocks …

Jaysus, time to drown the shamrock!

Shebeen (noun)

Depending on who you ask, this term comes from the Irish word *síbín* meaning illicit Irish whiskey or *seibin* meaning a small mug, and they both came from the older word *séibe* meaning mugful. And we have a lot to thank the shebeen for, as essentially it was the forerunner of the now ubiquitous Irish pub, and many a million, million mugfuls have been downed over the decades.

The original shebeens in Ireland began their life in the eighteenth century, mostly selling illicit whiskey after laws banned the sale of *poitín* and it moved underground. In

A Shebeen at Donnybrook by Erskine Nicol (1852).

fact, so much of it was sold in shebeens that a lot of the patrons ended up underground as well.

The Irish diaspora exported the idea of the shebeen all over the world, including to the UK, the US, Canada and a bunch of African nations. In South Africa, shebeens became a vital part of the fabric of life, thanks to a 1927 law banning black South Africans from entering a tavern. This gave birth the concept of the 'Shebeen Queens', black women who produced home-brew beer and sold it in secret drinking dens. During apartheid, the shebeen became the place for black people to meet and discuss politics and how to gain freedom from oppression.

The shebeen in Ireland enjoyed an unfortunate revival of sorts during the Covid pandemic. With pubs closed, some budding 'publicans' began setting up illegal shebeens around the country in caravans and sheds, allowing them to dispense booze, and spread cheer along with the potentially deadly virus.

The first appearance of the word shebeen in print was in a 1789 ballad called 'Kilmainham Minit': 'Wid de Stiff to a Shebeen we hied'. The song tells the tale of the hanging of a notorious criminal, his kicking legs resembling a new dance known as 'The Kilmainham Minuet'.

Dublin humour at its finest!

Sheila (noun)

The Aussie slang term for a girl or woman is as obvious as it looks – it derives from the Irish female name *Síle* and was most likely brought Down Under by Irish convicts who were deported for stealing a loaf of bread, or even stealing a crooked glance at their Sassenach overlords.

Originally the word was applied only to Irish females, but over the years it became a generic term for women, specifically by men, and was originally affectionate. In more recent decades, it came to be regarded in the same way as the British term 'birds', i.e. not quite PC. But now it seems Aussie women are reclaiming it, as evidenced by books such as *Sheilas: Badass Women of Australian History* by Eliza Reilly. Fair dinkum.

Shenanigans (noun)

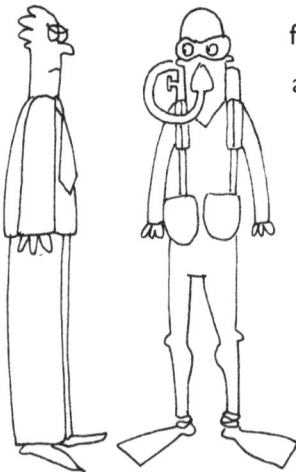

NO RON, THERE'S NO SUCH THING AS 'SCUBA DIVING FRIDAY'!

FECKIN' OFFICE SHENANIGANS!

This is a great word, useful for all sorts of stuff. When some dosser TD arranges for the new hospital to be built in his backyard, we call it political shenanigans. When a footballer pretends to be tripped and throws himself down like he's been hit with a feckin' howitzer round, it's sporting shenanigans. And when a pension provider has been using your funds to play the stock market, the phrase we'd reach for is lowlife scumbag. Sorry, I meant financial shenanigans. Then

there's drunken shenanigans, criminal shenanigans and, on a more positive note, sexy shenanigans, which usually involve odd-shaped vibrating toys, overhead mirrors, dripping chocolate, or see-through pink underwear (and that's just for the fellas). So shenanigans is certainly versatile in application.

Despite it sounding totally Irish, the origin of the term is something of a mystery, although there is every chance it's ours to claim. But in the interests of fairness, here are the opposing theories.

There are suggestions that it might originate from the French *ces manigances*, meaning fraudulent schemes (that's a big pile of French *merde* if you ask us). Another suggestion is from the Spanish *chanada*, meaning deceit (doesn't sound remotely like the word, so *vamos* to that idea). Then there's the German *Scheineilige*, meaning sham holy men (they can kiss that rubbish explanation *auf wiedersehen*).

And, of course, there's the most likely etymology from the Irish word *sionnachuighim* meaning 'I play the fox'. Not only does our Irish word sound most like *shenanigans* but its translation is the nearest to its actual meaning.

The word first appeared in print during the California Gold Rush in the mid-1850s, at which time, for example, one third of San Francisco's population was of recent Irish descent, which further backs up the Irish claim. And on top of all that evidence, it really does sound like an Irish word!

One way or the other, Irish publicans the world over have made their own minds up – there are roughly a gazillion Irish pubs dotted around the globe called 'Shenanigans'. So no more of these French/German/ Spanish shenanigans please.

Shillelagh (noun)

The logo of the Boston Celtics basketball team is (and how clichéd Irish is this?) a leprechaun wearing a shamrock-spotted hat and waistcoat while he leans on his shillelagh with one hand and spins a basketball with the other. Padderywhackery taken to its zenith!

Shillelaghs aren't that common in Ireland nowadays, except maybe as posh walking sticks but, in centuries gone by, they were considered vital for such things as

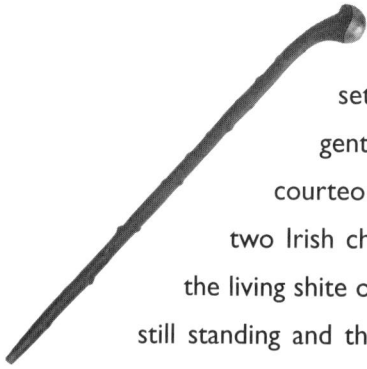

settling disputes by way of polite gentlemanly duels: acting in a very courteous and well-mannered way, the two Irish chaps would commence beating the living shite out of each other until one was still standing and the other was lying in a bloodied heap on the ground. Shillelaghs also came in handy for bashing in the brains of invading Sassenachs, and then as time passed, bashing in each other's brains when they were used in faction fights, or in organised brawls at fairs (see Donnybrook).

The diaspora brought them overseas where they were employed in much the same manner, i.e. to inflict destruction and death, which is probably why the Americans named the MG51 Shillelagh anti-tank missile and the aircraft of the 357th Fighter Group after them.

The word comes from the pretty little village of Shillelagh in south County Wicklow, where the original

TOP O' THE MORNIN' TO YE!

skull-smashing implements were sourced, and the village's name comes from a seventh-century clan chieftain called Ealach. His descendants, *Síol Ealaigh*, or 'seed of Ealach' gave us the term. His seed has spread far and wide indeed.

Sight for sore eyes (saying)

As recorded in previous entries, Jonathan Swift was a man who loved to take the mickey out of his contemporaries' corruption, immorality and general hoity-toity carry-on. Swift's speciality was cutting phrases such as 'It is remarkable with what Christian fortitude and resignation we can bear the suffering of other folks.' Or another good one, 'Laws are like cobwebs, which may catch small flies, but let wasps and hornets break through.' His 1738 book, *A Complete Collection of Genteel and Ingenious Conversation*, was a satirical take on the banality of conversation among the middle and upper classes. And within its pages we find the original version of what was to become a phrase that is still widely in use today: 'My Lord, methinks the sight of you is good for sore eyes.' The phrase was later shortened to 'a sight for sore eyes' and was soon in widespread and long-term use, such as in this joke by comedian Tom Vine: 'Conjunctivitis.com? Now that's a site for sore eyes!'

CONJUNCTIVITIS.COM
—A SITE FOR SORE EYES—

Skedaddle (verb)

OK, it's not certain by any means, but there are good grounds to suggest that skedaddle, meaning 'to get the hell out of here', is of Irish origin.

The term first made its appearance in print during the American Civil War. In 1862, a newspaper reported that, 'As soon as the rebs saw our red breeches … coming through the woods, they skedaddled.' It also appeared in Stephen Crane's Civil War novel, *The Red Badge of Courage:* 'Lots of good-a-'nough men have thought they was going to do great things before the fight, but when the time come they skedaddled.'

Sounds like there was a lot of skedaddling going on in the American Civil War.

Within a few years, the word had made its way across the Atlantic and also makes an appearance in James Joyce's *Ulysses:* 'Wheels within wheels. Police whistle in my ears still. All skedaddled.'

As a great many Irishmen fought on both sides in the American Civil War, it is possible that press reporters picked up a

phrase they were using to describe men fleeing the battle. The old Irish word *sgedadol*, meaning scatter or scattering, fits the meaning nicely and also sounds like the modern use of the term.

So, until etymologists come up with a better explanation, they can skedaddle off to their ancient dictionaries, because we're claiming it!

Slew (noun)

We have lots of slews in Ireland: slews of people waiting on hospital trolleys, slews of leaks in our water network, slews of gaps in public transport, slews of yobbos yobbing, slews of people who can't afford to buy or rent a home. And despite the fact that we also have slews of spare tax billions in the bank, we seem incapable of using these slews to fix any of the aforementioned slews.

The word slew, meaning 'a great many', finds its origin in

WHAT ARE WE WAITING FOR NOW?

PLEASE WAIT.

the Irish word *sluagh*, which translates as 'a crowd, a host or a great multitude'. It made its first appearance in print in the 1839 novel *Green Mountain Boys* by D.P. Thompson, and the casual usage suggests the word was fairly widespread at that point. Its appearance is not surprising as the novel is set in Vermont, a state that, in the mid-nineteenth century, attracted Irish immigrants by the slew.

Slob (noun)

One of the things about the Covid pandemic is that, to a large extent, it turned us all into slobs. Being essentially confined to our homes seemed a terrible burden at first, but we soon adapted by collapsing onto the settee with a beer in one hand and a bag of snacks in the other, and then proceeding to watch every episode of every series on Netflix, be they wonderful or plain wojus. Kilograms were gained by the dozen and general untidiness ensued – because 'why the hell should I bother showering or shaving when I'm not going to bleedin' see anyone?' Being a slob was feckin' deadly.

The term, meaning 'a slovenly and boorish person',

comes from the Irish word *slab*, which means 'mud, ooze, mire, muddy land,' thus equating slobbish people with mess, mud and general unpleasantness. The original meaning (i.e. muddy land) is also still in use today in places such as the North Slob Wildfowl Reserve in Wexford.

Arguably one of the biggest slobs in history was Henry VIII. In later life, his love of stuffing his gob, drinking himself legless and taking no exercise (apart from ordering his wives' heads to be separated from their bodies) resulted in his waist expanding to an impressive 138cm, or 54 inches (86cm, or 34 inches, is about average for a man). He got so unwieldy he needed a bunch of large guys to wheel or carry him around – not that it stopped him eating. He eventually developed a delightful condition where his body was covered in pus-filled boils. Truly the King of the Slobs.

Slogan (noun)

Guinness is good for you. Probably not, but that was officially the first-ever advertising slogan the brand employed in 1929. And that's what we mostly associate the word slogan with nowadays. Ads. You've heard thousands of them: 'Just do it', 'Probably the best lager in the world', 'Every little helps', 'Vorsprung durch Technik', 'Try Viagra – how hard can it be?' Okay, we admit, we made that last one up.

GOVERNMENT
RE-ELECTION CAMPAIGN

'WE NEED A CATCHY SLOGAN.
SOMETHING THAT WILL HIDE
OUR INCOMPETENCE.'

But slogans aren't what they used to be. This is not a statement decrying a downturn in the quality of advertising over the years. Back in the day in Ireland, Irish clans all had their own distinct *sluagh-ghairm*, which broke down as *sluagh*, meaning army and *ghairm*, meaning battle cry.

For example, the O'Neill clan's *sluagh-ghairm* was 'Red hand to victory!', which would be yelled by thousands of bloodthirsty warriors as they prepared to rearrange the enemy English soldiers' innards. The Fitzgeralds' *sluagh-ghairm* was 'In the glory of the old place!', the Kellys' was 'God is my tower!', and so on. These battle cries were a source of pride to the men and had a powerful unifying effect as they prepared for battle. They were so effective, in fact, that Henry VIII (see Slob) actually tried to outlaw them in 1537. No chance.

As the centuries passed, the term *sluagh-ghairm* became known in England and was eventually anglicised into slogan and it became the norm for clubs and institutions to adopt one that was a distillation of their 'philosophy'. As the twentieth century dawned, the slogan was hijacked by the advertising industry and now everything from cheesy-flavoured puffs to toilet rolls to underpants brands have their own distinctive slogans.

From 'Death before disgrace!' to 'Finger-lickin' good', how the mighty *sluagh-ghairm* has fallen.

Smidgen (noun)

There are reasonably good odds that this term originates from the Irish *smidirín* and the Scots Gaelic *smidean,* meaning fragment. There's also a smidgen of a chance that it came from the old English term *smeddum*, meaning fine powder, but the Sassenachs can feck off.

In Ireland, the word smidgen can be interpreted in multiple ways. For example,

a smidgen of a pay rise is, as you'd expect, stingy as feck, whereas when you tell your auntie that yes, you'll just have a smidgen more whiskey, she will then proceed to pour you enough booze to anaesthetise a horse.

And when you think about it, someone really missed a trick by not deciding the name of a baby pigeon was a smidgen.

Smithereens (noun)

The Irish word *smidirín* (see also Smidgen) is likely to be the origin of smithereens, meaning tiny pieces. Certainly the earliest appearances in print were in Ireland. In 1795, the *Dublin Evening Post* reproduced a notice posted by local Orangemen on a magistrate's home in Enniscorthy:

Mr Pounden, – Sir, we gave you notice some
time ago to quit this country, for you are making

a rebellion here – we tell you now again, that
if you do not be off directly, by the gost [*sic*] of
William, and by the Orange we wear, we will
break your carriage in smithereens, and hoch your
cattle, and burn your house etc. …

No messin' with the Orange yobbos there, although they
clearly needed some spelling lessons.

The word was a favourite of Bugs Bunny's arch-enemy
Yosemite Sam who would frequently proclaim 'Ya better
say your prayers, ya flea-bitten varmint … I'm-a-gonna
blow ya to smithereens!' before Bugs pulled off some
masterstroke to outwit him. As a result of this, many
Americans assumed the Looney Tunes writers coined the
word. But no, Irish people had been blowing their enemies
to smithereens for centuries beforehand.

12 PINTS AND A VINDALOO LAST NIGHT. THE TOILET IS IN SMITHEREENS!

Snazzy (adj.)

The truth is that nobody really has a clue where this came from, but there are three main theories. One is that it's a combination of snappy and jazz, and was coined in the US around 1931. Maybe, but seems a bit like a wild guess. Another is that it comes from the English singer and raconteur George Snazel, who was referred to as Snazzy in a report in New Zealand's *Wellington Evening Post* in 1901, reputedly the first time the term appeared in print. But despite his rather dapper appearance, his nickname was, apparently, a mere coincidence.

And, of course, there's the theory that it comes from the Irish word *snas*, which means polish or good appearance, which is the snazziest explanation – from an Irish point of view!

YOU LOOK GREAT, HONEY. LIKE YOU'RE DRESSED TO KILL.

Spunk (noun)

No, it's not what you're thinking, you filthy pervert, but rather the term that means courage, spirit and determination. Or to show a lot of guts. Actually, it's a word that sounds quite British, and you can easily imagine some stuffy, moustachioed army officer back

HE SURE HAD A LOT OF GUTS.

in the day exclaiming 'I say, old boy, our gallant soldiers fought with unsurpassed spunk!'

Spunky-looking lot

But the word actually derives from the old Irish word *sponnc*, meaning tinder. From that we can extrapolate to spark, courage and inner spirit, i.e. spunk. The term has fallen out of common usage thanks, one would suppose, to its associations with the slang term for something quite different. Nobody wants the embarrassment of being misunderstood on that one!

Steeplechase (noun)

On one day every year people all over Ireland and Britain reach for the Saturday newspaper, open the sports pages and stick a pin in the long list of names that details the runners and riders in the Aintree Grand National. Either that or they pick a horse not because of its form or its jockey but because it has a cute-sounding name like 'Pink Petal', or an unintentionally crude one like 'Hoof Hearted', or a plain wojus one like 'Maythehorsebewithu'. They'll then trot nervously into

MY HORSE CAME IN AT 20 TO 1.

BRILLIANT!

HARDLY. THE OTHERS FINISHED THE RACE AT 12.30.

THE GRAND NATIONAL STEEPLE-CHASE

the local bookies and place '€5 each way' on a complete no-hoper, while the regulars there snigger behind their back at their cluelessness.

What most people don't know is that the Aintree race (and all other horsing steeplechases), along with the Olympic running version, all owe their beginnings to an event that took place in Ireland in 1752. One night, a certain Cornelius O'Callaghan and one Edmund Blake were at dinner at Buttevant Castle in County Cork, discussing their passion for riding and racing and getting rat-arsed in the process, when they decided to have a little wager. They would race across country between the two most visible objects on the local landscape – the steeple of St John's Church in Buttevant and that of St Mary's Church in Doneraile, a distance of four miles. And thus the word steeplechase was born, along with the new sport. Word spread faster than a TD can fill an expenses claim, and soon half of Ireland's horse riders were leaping ditches and vaulting over streams as the new craze caught on. Pretty soon, the British and French were at it and in 1839 the first Aintree steeplechase was held.

Incidentally, among the many other words that have their origin in Irish drunken conversations are 'Goanask-mebollix' and 'Justafu**inbout'.

Huntsman Cornelius O'Callaghan.

Sudocrem (noun)

It has almost become a generic term for a healing skincare ointment the world over. But it began its life in 1931, when Professor of Pharmacy Thomas Smith of Dublin, working in the back of his shop on Old Cabra Road, combined various soothing substances with a mild antiseptic and disinfectant, and produced the planet's favourite treatment for babies' sore bums, eczema, minor burns, chilblains and even the sunburn you get when you've over-exposed your milky-white Irish skin on Ireland's annual three day 'heatwave'.

NOTHING THAT A SMIDGE OF SUDOCREM WON'T SORT.

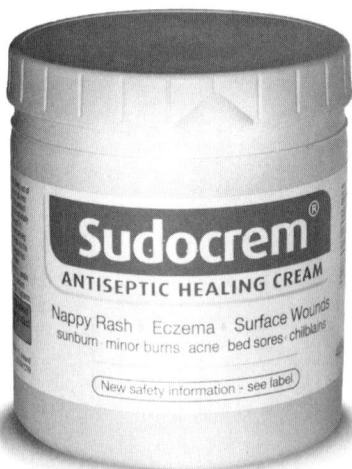

Actually, he originally named it 'Smith's Cream' after himself, later changing it to 'Soothing Cream', and he sold it out of his pharmacy to customers who were mostly from the neighbourhood. The locals were delighted with it, but the pharmacist noticed that whenever someone ordered it in their Dublin Northside accent, instead of 'Soothing Cream' they were actually saying '*Suda-cree-em*'. He loved the sound and duly changed it to the now familiar term.

Manufactured locally until recently, it quickly took off all over Ireland, then the UK and then the world.

It truly is the *crème de la crème* of healing creams.

Superman (noun)

Yes, it's hard to credit that the man in the blue jumpsuit and red cloak wearing his underwear on the outside, who can leap buildings in a single bound, owes his name to an Irishman, one George Bernard Shaw.

Shaw coined the term for his 1903 play *Man and Superman*, a sort of highbrow philosophical romcom that takes digs at the society of the day, and man and woman's supposed place therein. He borrowed a concept previously created by

the German philosopher Friedrich Nietzsche in 1883, *Übermensch*, which translates as 'above man or above human'. Shaw came up with his own translation – superman – and the word duly entered the English language.

In 1938, writer Jerry Siegel and artist Joe Shuster borrowed the term as the name for a character they'd created for DC Comics, and Superman as we know him was born. Unfortunately, the creators received just $130 for the exclusive rights. Which sort of makes the Man of Steel's slogan seem quite ironic: 'Truth and justice the American way!'

Tie the knot (saying)

In the ancient Celtic world, getting hitched involved the bride and groom being tied together during the ceremony, something they had probably planned to do anyway during their wedding night, but for different reasons. This was called handfasting and supposedly gives us the phrase 'tying the knot'.

It involved binding the couple's hands together during their vows as a symbol of the contract they were entering into and their eternal devotion to each other – in other words they'd be stuck with each other even if they ended up hating each other's guts. Supposedly the tradition goes back seven thousand years, but how you could possibly

NICE TO SEE SHE FINALLY TIED THE KNOT.

establish that is anyone's guess, as there has only been recorded history since about AD 400. For all we know, wedding ceremonies seven millennia ago involved bathing in pig's blood before being rolled in soot then dangled upside down from a tree while the chieftain tickled the pair with chicken feathers.

Handfasting is not unique to Celtic Ireland or Scotland, and there are similar ceremonies practised in China and India, but the phrase 'tying the knot' probably evolved from the custom here.

With some handfasting ceremonies, the couple's hands would only be untied after they'd consummated the union. One would assume this required a witness or two to be present while 'Willy Winkle explored the hidden valley', to employ a creepy euphemism of old. Either that or *post coitus* they'd have to yell out from the bridal suite to the assembled guests outside, 'Right, all done now, come and untie us!' Either way, those ancients were pretty kinky head-the-balls.

Tory (noun, adj.)

Considering how pig-ignorant most of the UK's Tory party are about Irish historical matters, it's quite likely that most of them have little or no idea how they came to be known as Tories in the first place, and the fact that their nickname implies they're a bunch of yobbos. You have to go back to the mid-seventeenth century to track down the origin of the word in the English language.

You see, in the sixteenth and seventeenth centuries, when the Brits basically nicked most of our lands, many of the Irish peasantry were forced to take to the hills and woods where some became bandits, frequently raiding the lands and homes of the settlers, and occasionally turning their innards into their outards. And who could blame them? Wasn't a decent English disembowelling a great way to raise the spirits! These gangs became known as *toraidhe* or *toruighe*, meaning outlaws. As the years passed the term was anglicised and became a general insult.

FAREWELL, AND THANKS FOR ALL THE MONEY!

144

During the Exclusion Crisis of 1678, bills were introduced to exclude King Charles II's brother, James II, from the throne because he was a Catholic. In the dispute, two new parties formed, and one was given the insulting nickname of Tory, because they were seen as political outlaws. These boyos would go on to form today's modern Conservative Party. So basically, the party and its members are named after a shower of savages and backstabbers.

Fits the modern Tories like a glove.

Trousers (noun)

Trousers have been around a long time and archaeologists have discovered what are thought to be the oldest pair of trousers, dating from 3000 BC in China. Historians seem to agree that trousers came into fashion for men thanks to the widespread adoption of the horse as a means of transport – basically, it was too uncomfortable having one's exposed nuts bouncing up and down on the horse's back.

In medieval times,

MY MISSUS WEARS THE TROUSERS IN OUR HOUSE

trousers were originally a tight-fitting, body-hugging garment, evolving to a design that ballooned out over the thighs so that it looked like you had a pair of pumpkins shoved down your pants. It wasn't until the nineteenth century after the Industrial Revolution that, probably for practical reasons, they took on an appearance more resembling today's designs.

Although primarily a men's garment, women in Persia and other places in the ancient world wore trousers, but a woman donning trousers in the West was considered outrageous in the nineteenth century. Many US cities had laws banning the practice well into the twentieth century, until Amelia Bloomer put her foot down in 1851 and created a fashion for a loose trouser for women, known as bloomers. Men obviously felt threatened in the trouser department.

The word 'trousers' derives from the Middle Irish term *triubhas*, which evolved into 'trouzes' and gradually entered the English language. It is mentioned in *A Challenge for Beauty*, a 1636 play by Englishman Thomas Heywood:

I am clean out of love with your Irish trouzes;

they are for all the world like a jealous wife,

always close at a man's tayle!

Truant (noun)

One of the world's most famous truants was the great Marlon Brando, who said of himself: 'I was a bad student, chronic truant and all-around incorrigible.'

He was frequently absent from school, threw firecrackers in the building, submitted an essay written on a roll of toilet paper and rode a motorcycle through the school corridors. If you're going to get expelled, might as well do it in style.

In fact, lots of famous people were guilty of truancy, including author Jackie Collins, singer Courtney Love, Beatle John Lennon and physicist Albert Einstein!

The word probably comes via the old French word *truand*, meaning rogue/beggar, which itself came from the old Irish *trógán/trúag*, meaning wretch/wretched, which, appropriately, is how repeated truancy leaves most truants.

Despite the term having distant Celtic origins, modern Ireland has generally used the term mitching to describe truancy, and most

SCHOOL IS FOR MUGS

Albert Einstein (1879–1955).

people believe this is an Irish slang word. In fact, it is also very popular in parts of England and originally comes from another French word: *muchier*, meaning 'to hide'.

Back in the old days, kids were warned about the 'Mitching Man', a dark and mysterious figure who spent his days in hot pursuit of truant kids. Thoughts of this guy nabbing you would put the fear of Jaysus into most, because if he caught you he'd reputedly box the head off you, before dragging you back to school where they'd box the head off you again, after which you'd be sent home and have your head boxed off you a third time for bringing shame on the family. Mitching, not surprisingly, was pretty rare.

Truism (noun)

Jonathan Swift again. A truism can be defined as a self-evident truth or a statement that is generally accepted as obviously true, such as 'if we're to stop hospital overcrowding, we'll need more beds.' Truism made its first appearance in 1708 in Swift's satirical essay, 'Remarks Upon a Book entitled *The Rights of the Christian Church*'.

DO YOU SWEAR TO TELL THE TRUISM, MR SWIFT?

Of course there are supposed truisms that are obviously untrue, like 'Time heals all wounds' (unless, for example, you've just had a leg amputated). Is this an example of an 'untruism'?

Anyway, some other truism examples:

If you don't know where you are going,
    you'll end up someplace else.
It was all so different before everything changed.
All the lies in the party's manifesto simply aren't true.
Beginning a sentence, 'Now, don't get angry
    …' will always have the reverse effect.
Never ever mix sleeping pills and laxatives.
If at first you don't succeed, then
    skydiving definitely isn't for you.

Turn a deaf ear (saying)

Even more Jonathan Swift! This phrase, meaning 'to blatantly ignore what someone is saying', can be pretty much attributed to Swift. However, the term 'deaf' makes several earlier appearances in the Bible where it means 'to ignore' as opposed to 'is as deaf as a post'. But possibly the earliest recorded written use of the phrase 'turn a deaf ear' is found in Swift's 1724 poem 'Dingley and Brent':

> Should Solomon wise
> In majesty rise,
> And show them his wit and his learning;
> They never would hear,
> But turn the deaf ear,
> As a matter they had no concern in.

The poem is named for Swift's housekeeper, Brent, and Rebecca Dingley, the companion of Esther Johnson (nick-named Stella, and Swift's one true love), and concerned their seeming inability to listen. Swift and Stella never married. Maybe his proposals fell on deaf ears?

Twig (see Dig)

Vector (noun)

A quick reminder to anyone who wasn't paying attention as their scruffy, beardy maths teacher (they were all
scruffy and beardy, even the women) droned on during
geometry lessons about vectors: a vector is a quantity that
has both size and direction. The word is a direct lift from
the Latin *vecto,* which means 'to carry/to convey' and Irish
astronomer and mathematician William Rowan Hamilton
first coined it in the mathematical sense in 1846.

Hamilton was a bit of a genius, and you owe him more
than you probably imagine. Next time you're sitting in front
of the telly watching a dinosaur bite someone's head off or
a spacecraft crashing into the Great Pyramid of Giza, well,
first consider that you really should improve the quality
of your movie choices, and second, that the special effects
computer wizardry is largely thanks to Hamilton giving the
world quaternion algebra. This is a complex mathematical
concept that deals with mechanics in three-dimensional
space (trust us, don't try to grasp it any further than that!).
His theories also played a major part in space exploration,
optics and the control systems of planes.

On 16 October 1843, Hamilton and his wife, Helen,

were walking along the banks of the Royal Canal in Dublin, she no doubt talking about the latest styles in horsehair petticoats and he nodding in agreement and muttering 'yes, undoubtedly, oh definitely', while his brain was a billion miles away, when he suddenly had a moment of startling inspiration, stopped beneath Broome Bridge (a plaque still marks the spot) and scratched the formula for quaternion algebra on the underside with a penknife:

$$i^2 = j^2 = k^2 = ijk = -1$$

Well, that's pretty obvious really when you think about it.

Wellington (boot) (noun)

Although the Duke of Wellington is widely celebrated as an English war hero and two-time prime minister of Britain, he was, in fact, Irish, whether he liked it or not. Arthur Wellesley, to give him his name at birth, generally identified as British, especially when in England, which may have been for political reasons, since being Irish at the time was regarded as something of a liability, we being such a trouble-some bunch.

Regarding his nationality, he was erroneously attributed with a famous quotation about how being born in a stable didn't make one a horse. However, this was more likely said *about* the duke by none other than the Liberator, Daniel O'Connell: 'The poor old duke, what shall I say of him? To be sure he was born in Ireland, but being born in a stable does not make a man a horse.'

Anyway, the fact is that he was born in Merrion Street, Dublin, in 1769, lived his childhood in County Meath, and served in the Irish Parliament as MP for Trim. And in the Phoenix

Wellington Monument, Dublin.

Park you'll see the largest obelisk in Europe, erected in his memory, which many Irish people would like to see go the way of Nelson's Column, thanks to Wellington's colonial, imperialist attitudes.

But to the wellies: in the late eighteenth century, British soldiers wore boots called Hessians, made from calfskin and featuring poncy tassels. In the early nineteenth century, the Duke asked his shoemaker to modify the boots using softer calfskin that rose to the knee and also to remove the tassels. By the time he'd played a part in Napoleon's defeat in 1815, the war hero had made the boots very fashionable, and every gentleman was keen to be seen out and about sporting what became known as 'Wellington Boots'. It's hard to imagine these guys sitting in a fancy London restaurant or doing a waltz with some lady while wearing wellies, but there you go.

By the twentieth century, everyone wanted them, even the great unwashed, so they began mass-producing the boots using rubber.

Who knows, perhaps they'll become fashionable again among society's movers and shakers, and we'll see the likes of the Taoiseach strolling out at an EU summit sporting green wellies, or even better, Saoirse Ronan on the Oscars red carpet with pink wellies. You read it here first!

Whiskey (noun)

Each day billions of people around the world order a whiskey (or ten), not realising that what they're actually saying is the Irish term for 'water of life', i.e. *uisce beatha*.

It's ironic that something that will clearly melt your innards if consumed in too great a quantity has its name origin in a term that sounds like a beverage you'd buy from a health-food guru.

Most people around the globe mistakenly believe that whiskey originated in Scotland. As the Scots would say: 'Och, yer bum's oot the windae!' (translation: 'That's rubbish talk!'). The fact is that the earliest written record of the term whiskey is from the Annals of Clonmacnoise, which recounts how some eejit chieftain in 1405 got so gee-eyed on the stuff that he killed himself. The first record in Scotland is from ninety years later. On top of

I AIN'T HEARING YOU RIGHT, PARDNER. DID YOU SAY WHISKEY OR WHISKY?

that, Bushmills in County Antrim is the oldest whiskey distillery in the world, having been granted its licence to distil in 1608. So up yer kilt, Scotty!

Besides all that, Irish whiskey is triple distilled to create a smooth, magical nectar that glides off the tongue, leaving a heavenly afterburn on the throat, whereas Scotch leaves you feeling like someone's throttling you. (Seriously, though, Scotch is a fine drink, just somewhat rougher around the edges. Think Aston Martin v VW Beetle. Haha.)

The other difference between Irish and Scotch is, of course, that Irish whiskey is spelled with an 'e' as opposed to Scottish whisky. Conor McGregor and his team were clearly unaware of this fact when he tried to launch his 'Notorious Irish Whisky' back in 2017. Anyway, they fixed it with the subsequent rebranding. Maybe they were all punch drunk with the excitement?

Wunderkind (noun)

These are those precocious, annoying little feckers you see crop up on YouTube or TikTok every now and then and make you feel totally inadequate, as they perform a Beethoven piano concerto flawlessly, or solve complex mathematical problems at lightning speeds, or balance a spinning ball on their nose while surfing, all at the age of six. There have been ganseyloads of *wunderkinder* (to use the correct plural) down the ages, including Mozart (who could play the harpsichord at three and was composing by five),

Picasso (who could draw before he could talk), our own William Rowan Hamilton (who, although a mathematician, had mastered Persian, Arabic, Malay, Sanskrit and Hindustani by thirteen), physicist Marie Curie (who had taught herself to read French and Russian by age four), and many more.

Of course, most wouldn't have been called *wunderkind* because the term entered the English language only in 1891, thanks once more to George Bernard Shaw adapting a German phrase for English use, except this time he obviously couldn't

be bothered translating it. *Wunderkind* literally translates as 'wonder child' but sounds much snappier in German. The first written use in English was in the weekly newspaper *The World*, to which Shaw was a regular contributor: 'Every generation produces its infant Raphaels and infant Rosciuses, and *Wunderkinder* who can perform all the childish feats of Mozart.'

Since then, it has come into widespread use – even the likes of Elon Musk has been described as a *wunderkind*. Jaysus. From Mozart to Musk. *Wunderkinder* ain't what they used to be.

But while we're here, Shaw was also responsible for several other, perhaps less well-known words, including 'Shavian', referring to his own life and works – he disliked the original 'Shawian', as it was a bit of a mouthful. He also was the first to shorten the word 'executive' to 'exec' and the word 'proletariat' to 'prole'. Then there's the lovely word 'moodle', which means 'to dawdle aimlessly or to idle time away', and deserves more frequent modern use, such as 'the people who control Ireland's major infrastructure projects are a right bunch of moodlers'. Another cracker is 'flagellomania', which describes those partial to an oul' whipping. And lastly, there's 'comstockery', which refers to the censorship of material that is considered sinful or obscene. As far as we're concerned, comstockers should go and **** themselves up the **** until they're well and truly ****ed.

Yahoo (noun, exclamation)

Jonathan Swift has made numerous contributions to this great tome, so it is fitting that he should have the privilege of making the final entry. 'Yahoo' is a word with multiple meanings including:

A brute in human form, aka a yobbo/ scumbag/hooligan/lout/bowsie.

A loud exclamation, usually of joy

An American web services provider based in California.

In Swift's *Gulliver's Travels* (1726), the eponymous hero ends up in the Land of the Houyhnhnms, who are a race of wise and civilised horses, but who share their home with another race called the Yahoos, who are human-like in appearance but savage, brutish, smelly and as thick as shite, much like modern-day yahoos. Swift was probably having a go here at his fellow humans and our capacity for brutality and stupidity despite our supposedly civilised nature.

Yahoo, when it means 'to exclaim', probably comes from the same source, it being the brutish sound made by the

creatures, although there is an argument that this meaning of yahoo comes from an old Native American word, meaning wolf. In other words, when someone shouted 'Yahoo!', it wasn't in joy but more of an exclamation of fear and warning, i.e. 'Oh shit!'

The company known as Yahoo is officially an acronym for 'Yet Another Hierarchical Officious Oracle' (Jaysus, what a brutal name!), but the founders Jerry Yang and David Filo said that they chose the term because, in the university they attended, it was used to refer to rude, unsophisticated and uncouth people, which brings us full circle back to Swift's Yahoos.

The end.

Yahoo!